HOOD'S
TENNESSEE
CAMPAIGN

JAMES R. KNIGHT

HOOD'S TENNESSEE CAMPAIGN

The Desperate Venture of a Desperate Man

THE
History
PRESS

Published by The History Press
Charleston, SC 29403
www.historypress.net

Cover: "General Forrest at Carnton," courtesy of John Paul Strain.

First published 2014

Manufactured in the United States

ISBN 978.1.62619.597.4

Library of Congress CIP data applied for.

Contents

Author's Foreword

Hood's Tennessee Campaign was a huge undertaking, involving at least eighty thousand combat troops marching and fighting over almost five thousand square miles of Middle Tennessee countryside for almost six weeks. For the people of Middle Tennessee, it was the most significant event of the Civil War that they witnessed personally. Obviously, a work of this scope can only hope to provide a brief overview of this, the Confederacy's last major offensive. Unfortunately, that means that most of the campaign's major events and most interesting characters will get much less attention than they deserve. Please see Sources and Suggested Reading for more details on specific parts of the campaign.

There are many excellent works that examine one area or another of the campaign, and I have tried to consult as many as I could. For the backbone of the story, however, I relied primarily on three sources:

Eric Jacobson's *For Cause and for Country*, which has become the standard reference for the early part of the campaign, especially from the Tennessee River through Spring Hill and Franklin.

James Lee McDonough's *Nashville: The Western Confederacy's Final Gamble*, which examines both armies' operations during the first two weeks of December 1864 and gives details of the two-day battle.

Derek Smith's *In the Lion's Mouth*, which details the one-hundred-mile-long retreat back to the Tennessee River.

For the multitude of detail about the armies and their operations and the communications of all the major figures, the *Official Records*, Volume 45, Parts I and II, were open on my desk and my computer constantly.

There are always people to thank, and as this is my fourth book in the Sesquicentennial Series, they are mostly the usual suspects. First and foremost, I'd like to thank all the folks at the Battle of Franklin Trust (BOFT), which operates the Carter House and Carnton Plantation in Franklin, Tennessee, for being a joy to work with and giving an old retired guy such a great part-time job. It also came in handy that Eric Jacobson, my friend and my boss at BOFT, knows more about this campaign than anybody else I know.

Brian Allison, former historian at the Travellers Rest Historic Site in Nashville, answered a lot of questions and once gave an impromptu seminar for myself and a Civil War buff from New Zealand over lunch. Brian was also my "go-to guy" for details and statistics on the Battle of Nashville.

Finally, thanks to the folks at The History Press for letting an old retired FedEx pilot try it one more time.

James R. Knight
Franklin, TN

Prologue

…the widest river in the world.

BAINBRIDGE, ALABAMA—MIDNIGHT, DECEMBER 28, 1864

It was dark and cold that night as Nathan Bedford Forrest began sending the men of his ad hoc command across the Tennessee River on a pontoon bridge. A week earlier, at Columbia, Tennessee, Confederate general John Bell Hood had made one of the best decisions of his career by putting Forrest in charge of covering the last sixty-five miles of the Army of Tennessee's retreat from the disaster at Nashville. With a cobbled-together force of his cavalry and some infantry led by Major General Edward Cary Walthall—fewer than five thousand men in all—Forrest had fought four critical delaying actions over the last five days, buying Hood the time he needed to save what was left of his army. Now, with his rear guard responsibilities completed, it only remained for Forrest to save his own men from the pursuing Federal forces.

The pontoon bridge that lay in front of Forrest's men was a rickety affair at best, but for the last day and a half, it had held together, giving Hood's army a means to reach the relative safety of the south bank of the river. Now, Forrest's troopers were told to dismount and lead their horses across, and one of them later said that the bridge seemed "as if it were nothing but inch boards laid on top of the water." Another, who had an injured leg and elected to stay mounted that night, said that the bridge was "in a swing, jumping up and down," and that the Tennessee seemed to be "the widest river in the world."[1]

By the middle of the day on the twenty-eighth, the last Confederates were across the river, and the engineers had cut the pontoons loose from the north bank. The nearest Federal troops—a special cavalry unit under Colonel George Spalding of the Twelfth Tennessee Cavalry—were still a few miles away. So ended the last Confederate offensive of the Civil War. The war in the Deep South would continue for another five months or so, but the Confederate Army of Tennessee was, for all intents and purposes, finished. The name remained, and many of its battered units and senior officers would fight on until the end with other commands, but the old Army of Tennessee that had fought at places like Stones River, Chickamauga, Missionary Ridge, Atlanta, Franklin and Nashville never took the field again.

Fifty-eight days earlier, when it began to arrive on the Tennessee River at Tuscumbia and Florence, Alabama, the Confederate Army of Tennessee was only a shadow of the force that had opposed Major General William T. Sherman's Federal army in northern Georgia at the beginning of the Atlanta Campaign, six months earlier. During that brutal summer, first under General Joseph E. Johnston and then under General John Bell Hood, its current commander, the army had lost northern Georgia, the city of Atlanta and almost half of its combat force. As they settled into camps on both sides of the Tennessee River at the beginning of November—ragged, hungry, exhausted and, in many cases, barefoot—the men resembled nothing so much as an army of homeless people. Even so, the nucleus of a veteran fighting force remained and was still quite dangerous.

In recent years, Hood's Tennessee Campaign has come to be viewed by many as a hopeless enterprise that was doomed from the beginning—a sort of quixotic dream of a delusional commander seeking to restore past glories. In early November 1864, however, the presence of Hood's army on the Tennessee River, just over one hundred air miles from the defenses at Nashville, was taken very seriously by everyone on the Northern side, from Major General George Thomas, commanding at Nashville, to General Grant and the rest of the Federal high command.

The reason the threat of an offensive by Hood's army was viewed with some alarm by the Federal high command was simple. The Army of Tennessee began to arrive at Florence and Tuscumbia, Alabama, on October 31, and ragged as it was, Hood could still field about thirty thousand effective troops. When joined by Nathan Bedford Forrest's cavalry, that number would rise to at least thirty-three thousand men of all arms—many of them hardened combat veterans. On November 1, there was no Federal force in Middle Tennessee that could have opposed an army of the size Hood could muster.

In early November, the threat of a Confederate army marching virtually unopposed on Nashville—which George Thomas held with only six to eight thousand garrison troops—seemed very real. If Nashville should fall, central Kentucky all the way to the Ohio River would then be wide open to Hood's presumably resupplied and revitalized army. This would be a disaster and would force a change in Washington's strategy, possibly even reducing the pressure on Lee at Richmond. This, at least, was what Hood, P.G.T Beauregard (Hood's department commander) and Jefferson Davis hoped would happen. All of them understood that it was a long-odds gamble, but in November 1864, long-odds gambles were about all the Confederacy had left.

Whatever some modern historians might think, Hood's Tennessee Campaign was not viewed by his superiors or the Federal commanders who opposed him as a fool's errand led by an incompetent commander who was out of touch with reality. To Union commanders in Tennessee—like George Thomas, John Schofield and David Stanley—and even Ulysses S. Grant, far away in Virginia, it was a very real threat and a critical battle they could not afford to lose. Some years after the war, General Grant was quoted as saying, "If I had been in Hood's place, I would have gone to Louisville and on north…I was never so anxious during the war as at that time."[2]

To Jefferson Davis, P.G.T. Beauregard and John Bell Hood, the Tennessee Campaign was the last realistic chance they had to blunt the Federal momentum, currently represented by William Sherman's coming "March to the Sea," which was choking the Confederacy to death. Surprisingly, in spite of the long odds, the campaign—at least until Franklin—would turn out to be, as the Duke of Wellington is often misquoted as saying of the Battle of Waterloo, "a damn close run thing."[3]

Chapter 1

The Army of Tennessee

The solemn-looking fifty-six-year-old gentleman who stepped off the train in this small Georgia town that rainy Sunday had one of the most difficult jobs in the world. His name was Jefferson Finis Davis, and he was the president of the Confederate States of America. For all but two months of its three-and-a-half-year existence, his country had been at war, and now, in the fall of 1864, it was fighting for its life. That summer had gone badly almost everywhere, but even though the capital at Richmond was now under siege, Davis viewed the problems in the Army of Tennessee as serious enough to demand his personal attention.

Unlike his counterpart in the North, who had very little military experience of any kind, Jefferson Davis had seen war from both the operational and administrative sides. A graduate of West Point in 1828, Davis served on active duty for seven years before resigning to marry the daughter of his commanding officer. During the Mexican-American War, Davis raised a regiment called the Mississippi Rifles and served with distinction under his former father-in-law, Zachary Taylor.[1]

After the war with Mexico, Davis had gone to Washington as a senator from Mississippi and served as chairman of the Senate Committee on Military Affairs and later as secretary of war under Franklin Pierce. When Mississippi seceded, Senator Davis was ordered home and commissioned a major general by Governor J.J. Pettus. He was preparing to take command

Jefferson F. Davis, president, Confederate States of America. Davis promoted John Bell Hood to command the Army of Tennessee and reorganized its command structure before the Tennessee Campaign. *Library of Congress.*

of the state militia when he received word that he had been elected president by the Confederate Convention in Montgomery, Alabama. His wife said that he read the telegram like a man reading his death warrant. Instead of commanding troops in the field, as he would have preferred, Davis's fate was to guide the affairs of state from Richmond. Now, in the early fall of 1864, he was in Georgia to reorganize the Army of Tennessee and try to salvage something from the loss of Atlanta.

The Confederate Army of Tennessee had suffered from turmoil within its command structure for most of its existence. Following the army's defeat at Missionary Ridge in late 1863—and a near revolt by several of his senior subordinates—General Braxton Bragg, its stern and prickly original commander, resigned and was recalled to Richmond. Bragg became an advisor to his friend President Davis and was replaced by General Joseph E. Johnston. In May 1864, Major General William T. Sherman's Federal army began its push through northern Georgia toward Atlanta. By mid-July, the Army of Tennessee had fallen back almost to the outskirts of the city along Peach Tree Creek, and President Davis decided that the only hope of stopping the Federal advance was to replace General Johnston with a more aggressive commander. Within the Army of Tennessee, the only serious candidates were the two senior corps commanders: Lieutenant General William J. Hardee and Lieutenant General John Bell Hood.

By seniority, Hardee was the next officer in line for command. A twenty-six-year army veteran, Hardee had seen service in Mexico and on the Texas frontier, served as the commandant of cadets at West Point and written what became a standard work on infantry tactics. Hardee had taken over as temporary army commander when Bragg resigned and was offered the permanent position, but he turned it down in favor of General Johnston,

Left: General John Bell Hood, commander, Confederate Army of Tennessee. Hood took command in mid-July 1864, presided over the loss of Atlanta and developed the plan for the Tennessee Campaign. He led the army into Middle Tennessee and then back into Alabama after the defeat at Nashville. *Library of Congress*.

Right: Lieutenant General William J. Hardee, corps commander, Confederate Army of Tennessee. Hardee led a corps during the Atlanta Campaign but was passed over for command of the army in favor of the younger and less experienced but more aggressive Hood. Hardee was reassigned at his own request after Atlanta. *Library of Congress*.

who outranked him. Fifteen years older—and eleven months senior as a lieutenant general—Hardee was much more experienced than the thirty-three-year-old Hood, but he had already refused command of the army once. More importantly, Jefferson Davis and Braxton Bragg, his senior military advisor, who was no friend of Hardee, could see no indication that Hardee would be any more aggressive than Johnston had been. Davis believed that the fate of Atlanta rode on this decision, so Hardee was passed over in favor of the next officer in line—the dashing, young and aggressive but physically damaged John Bell Hood.[5]

Born in Kentucky, Hood had graduated from West Point in 1853 and served in California with the Fourth U.S. Infantry and in Texas with the newly formed Second U.S. Cavalry. When Kentucky remained neutral following the attack on Fort Sumter, Hood joined a Texas unit as a captain of cavalry but was soon promoted to colonel, commanding the Fourth Texas

Infantry. By the spring of 1862, he was a brigadier general leading what became known as Hood's Texas Brigade. With impressive performances at Gaines' Mill, Second Manassas and Antietam, Hood became one of the Confederacy's rising stars. Put out of action for almost two months by a wound to his left arm on the second day at Gettysburg, Hood was still able to rejoin the army in time to go with Longstreet's Corps to Chickamauga. While leading an attack that split the Federal army and sent half of it fleeing back to Chattanooga, he was wounded again and lost his right leg above the knee. In spite of his physical disabilities, by the spring of 1864, Hood was back commanding a corps in the Army of Tennessee under Joseph E. Johnston—and wearing a European-made artificial leg smuggled through the Federal blockade. Now, in mid-July, he found himself promoted to temporary full general—the youngest army commander in the war on either side—and charged with the almost impossible task of saving the city of Atlanta from a Federal army almost twice the size of his own.

Following President Davis's wishes, as well as his own natural inclination, John Bell Hood began a much more aggressive defense of Atlanta. Over the next six weeks, he launched several attacks on different parts of the Federal army, but in the end, he only succeeded in piling up more casualties. By the first of September, the Confederates were in danger of being cut off, so Hood ordered that the city be abandoned. The loss of Atlanta also meant the loss of vast amounts of supplies and war materiel that the Confederates were not able to move. Due to confusion, the army's reserve ordnance train was trapped in the city when Sherman cut the Macon Railroad, and twenty-eight rail cars full of ammunition had to be blown up.[6]

During the fight for Atlanta, Hood's relationship with William Hardee, already strained by Hood's promotion over him, grew worse. Hood complained to Richmond about Hardee's performance as his senior corps commander, and Hardee complained about what he saw as Hood's misuse of his men and the frightful casualties that resulted from Hood's aggressive attacks. In fact, there was probably some truth to both claims. By the time Davis arrived, Hardee was demanding a transfer, saying he could no longer serve under Hood. For his part, Hood had already written to Richmond requesting that Hardee be relieved. Clearly, one of them had to go.

President Davis spent three days conferring with the senior commanders of the Army of Tennessee, and several expressed the opinion that a new commander was needed. They suggested either the return of Joe Johnston or bringing in General P.G.T. Beauregard. After hearing them out, Davis made his decisions. General Hood was retained as the army's commander, and Lieutenant General William Hardee's request for a transfer was granted. He was sent to command the Department of South Carolina, Georgia and Florida, and Major General Benjamin Franklin Cheatham, Hardee's senior division commander, was given command of Hardee's old corps.[7] The Army of Tennessee's other two corps were now commanded by Lieutenant General Alexander P. Stewart and Lieutenant General Stephen D. Lee.

The other pressing matter that President Davis came to discuss was how to deal with Sherman's next move now that Atlanta had fallen. The prevailing opinion among the Southern officers was that he would either move southwest toward Mobile and the Gulf coast or east toward the Atlantic coast at Savannah or Charleston. In the meantime, however, everyone agreed that they must do something. Simply sitting and waiting for Sherman's next move would be disastrous in terms of desertions and troop morale. Accordingly, it was decided that Hood would take the army back north and operate against Sherman's supply line—the Western and Atlantic Railroad running south from Chattanooga. Besides keeping the army employed, the hope was that Sherman would come out of Atlanta with part of his army to protect his supply line and offer Hood a chance to attack him on favorable ground.

With the organization of the army and the next plan of action settled, President Davis started back for Richmond and General Hood got the army moving. On September 29, the army began crossing the Chattahoochee River, heading for Sherman's railroad. Hood had promised President Davis that he would "lay his claws" on Sherman's supply line and not let go until he provoked him into responding. President Davis, however, was not quite finished. On his way back to Richmond, he met with General P.G.T. Beauregard in Augusta, Georgia, and established the Military Division of the West, with Beauregard as its commander. This would make the Creole General Hood's immediate superior and hopefully add some supervision and support to the Army of Tennessee's efforts.

By the third of October, troops from A.P. Stewart's corps were on the Western and Atlantic at Big Shanty, where they captured the small Federal outpost and moved on to capture the garrison at Acworth the next day. Just as Hood had hoped, this caused Sherman to bring the bulk of his army out of Atlanta in pursuit. The main body of the Confederate army now moved west toward the Alabama line, while Major General Samuel French's division was left to deal with the larger Federal instillation at Allatoona. Unlike the first two small outposts, Allatoona was held by a reinforced Federal brigade commanded by Brigadier General John M. Corse, and it put up a tenacious

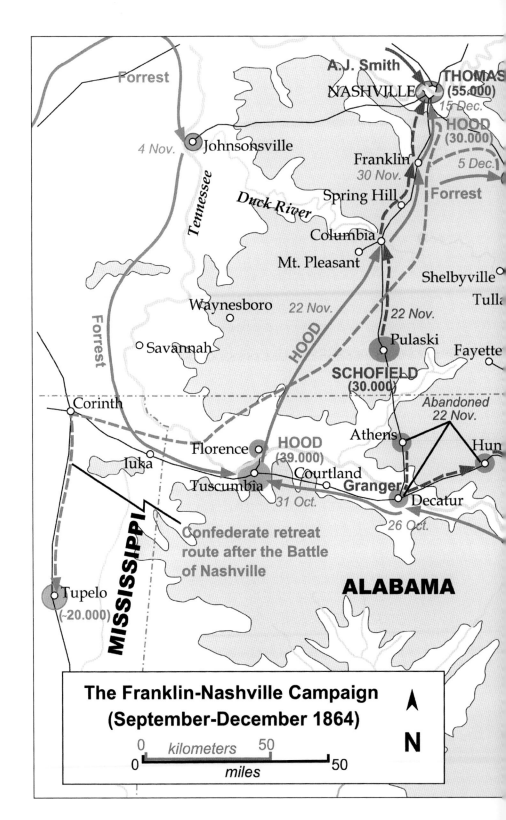

Forrest

A.J. Smith

NASHVILLE · THOMAS (55,000)
15 Dec.

4 Nov. ⊙ Johnsonville

HOOD (30,000)

Franklin
30 Nov.
5 Dec.

Tennessee

Duck River

Spring Hill

Forrest

Columbia

Mt. Pleasant

Shelbyville ○

Tulla

Forrest

Waynesboro ○

22 Nov.

HOOD

22 Nov.

○ Savannah

Pulaski

Fayette ○

SCHOFIELD (30,000)

○ Corinth

Abandoned
22 Nov.

Athens

Hun

Florence ○

HOOD (39,000)

Iuka ○

Courtland

Granger

Decatur

Tuscumbia

31 Oct.

26 Oct.

Confederate retreat
route after the Battle
of Nashville

MISSISSIPPI

ALABAMA

○ Tupelo
(~20,000)

The Franklin-Nashville Campaign
(September-December 1864)

0   kilometers   50

0   miles   50

N

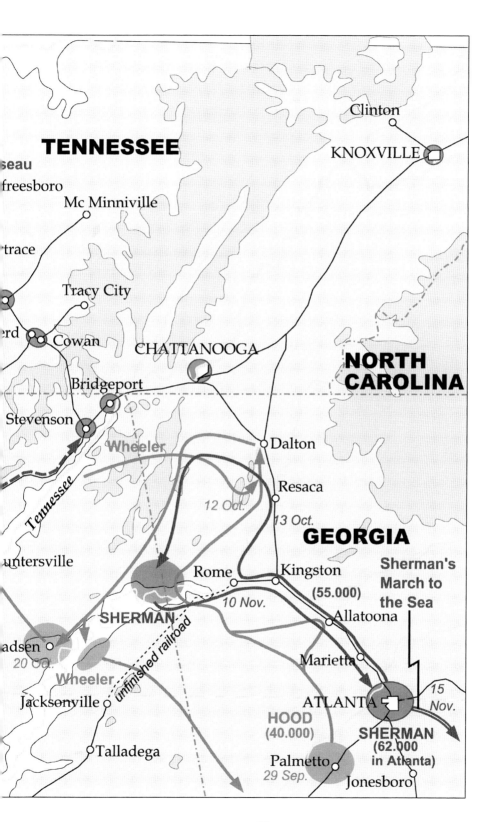

TENNESSEE

seau
freesboro
Mc Minniville
trace
Tracy City
rd Cowan
Bridgeport
Stevenson
Wheeler
Tennessee
untersville
SHERMAN
adsen
20 Oct.
Wheeler
Jacksonville
Talladega

CHATTANOOGA

Clinton
KNOXVILLE

NORTH
CAROLINA

Dalton
Resaca
12 Oct.
13 Oct.

GEORGIA

Rome Kingston
10 Nov. (55.000)
Allatoona
unfinished railroad
Marietta
ATLANTA
HOOD
(40.000)
Palmetto
29 Sep.
Jonesboro

Sherman's
March to
the Sea

15
Nov.

SHERMAN
(62.000
in Atlanta)

defense. Responding to a message from Sherman, who was sending troops to his relief, Corse, who had been wounded in the face, replied, "I am short a cheek-bone and an ear, but am able to whip all hell yet." True to his word, Corse continued to hold out, and French finally withdrew that afternoon and followed the rest of the army to the west.

By October 9, General Beauregard had caught up with Hood's army near Cave Springs, Georgia, and had his first meeting with his new subordinate. After being assured that Hood was still following the plan agreed on with President Davis, Beauregard left for the Gadsden, Alabama area to set up a supply base, and Hood took the army farther north to strike the Western & Atlantic at Resaca and Dalton. During the next ten days, Sherman could never catch up with the fast-moving Confederates, and Hood never found a place where he was willing to turn and force a fight.

By the twentieth, Hood had fallen back to Gadsden, Alabama, and the next day, he again met with Beauregard. At this meeting, Beauregard learned that Hood had a new plan. He wanted to move north to the Tennessee River; cross at Guntersville; attack the Federal positions on the Memphis & Charleston Railroad at Stevenson and Bridgeport, Alabama; and then turn north toward Nashville.

While this new plan was audacious, to be sure—and a complete departure from what Hood had agreed to with President Davis three weeks earlier—Beauregard felt it had promise if it could be executed quickly.[8] Beauregard did have one condition, however. Hood must leave most of his cavalry, under Major General Joe Wheeler, in northern Georgia to continue to harass Sherman's supply line. To replace Wheeler's cavalry, Beauregard promised Hood the services of Nathan Bedford Forrest and his men, whom he believed to be camped around Corinth, Mississippi. With Beauregard's approval—or at least his acquiescence—Hood moved his army out the next morning toward the Tennessee River at Guntersville, over thirty miles away. By the next day—without consulting Beauregard or anybody else—Hood had changed the plan again. Rather than try and force a crossing at Guntersville, he decided instead to turn west.

Sherman observed Hood's movements from his camp about thirty miles east of Gadsden, but when Hood marched off to the north, Sherman refused to follow. Having chased Hood all over north Georgia for the last three weeks, the Ohio general had had enough. He sent his Fourth Corps—about fourteen thousand men under Major General David Stanley—to Chattanooga to report to Major General George Thomas, whom Sherman had sent back to Nashville to be in charge of the defense of Tennessee,

Major General William T. Sherman, commander, Federal Military Division of the Mississippi. Sherman defeated the Army of Tennessee at Atlanta, left George Thomas in charge in Nashville and provided the troops whom Hood would face at Spring Hill and Franklin. *Library of Congress.*

and marched the rest of the army back toward Atlanta. A few days later, Sherman would also send the Twenty-third Corps—ten thousand men under Major General John Schofield—back to Tennessee as well. It would be these two corps, thrown together into an ad hoc little army of about twenty-five thousand men, that would, in a few weeks, oppose Hood in Middle Tennessee.

As the Confederates entered the valley of the Tennessee River and began to march westward, looking for a place to cross, the spirits of some of the men began to rise. A young staff officer in Lieutenant General A.P. Stewart's corps said that he was "glad to see that we are gradually getting into country where the women are more patriotic, prettier, & use less snuff than in certain portions of N. Ga."[9] Hood's immediate problem was finding a place to cross the Tennessee River, and on the afternoon of October 26, he arrived in Decatur, Alabama, where the crossing was guarded by a Federal garrison commanded by Brigadier General Robert Granger. After two days of skirmishing, however, Hood decided to bypass Decatur and march farther west.

On October 30, the leading elements of S.D. Lee's corps crossed the Tennessee River, chased away some Federal cavalry and occupied Florence, Alabama. The next day, Hood's other two corps, under A.P. Stewart and Frank Cheatham, arrived across the river near Tuscumbia and went into camp. The Confederates had been campaigning hard for the last month—their rations were scant, their bodies exhausted and their uniforms threadbare. As the troops settled in to rest, however, the planning for what became Hood's Tennessee Campaign began in earnest.

Chapter 2

The Tennessee River to Columbia

From the time that John Bell Hood made his new proposal to General Beauregard to cross the Tennessee River, an advance through Middle Tennessee to the Nashville area had always been part of the plan. Now that he and his army were eighty miles or so west of their planned crossing point, however, several things had changed, including the army's logistic situation.

The large supply base that General Beauregard had worked to establish near Gadsden was now over one hundred miles away by poor roads. It had to be abandoned and everything moved via the Mobile & Ohio Railroad and on to Corinth, Mississippi. Unfortunately, from there, the Memphis & Charleston was only serviceable eastward to Cherokee, Alabama. All the supplies had to then be hauled the last fifteen miles or so to Tuscumbia in rickety wagons pulled over miserable roads by decrepit horses and mules. This cobbled-together supply line had to support almost forty thousand men in the camps around Tuscumbia and Florence, as well as build up a stockpile of rations and munitions for the offensive to come. Hood had hoped to leave on the campaign with twenty days' rations for the men. He eventually marched north with about seven days' rations, and with the feeble Confederate supply system, he was lucky to have that.[10]

As at Gadsden, overseeing the logistic effort at Tuscumbia fell to General Beauregard, and he correctly laid the blame for much of his difficulties on General Hood and President Davis. After the war, Beauregard would write: "It was easy to discover in the details of the plan evidences of the fact that General Hood and Mr. Davis were not accustomed to command armies in the field, especially armies like ours...much had to be foreseen and much prepared or created."[11]

One thing that Beauregard and Hood agreed on, however, was the need for speed. On November 1, Middle Tennessee lay open to Hood's army, but it would not stay that way for long. When Hood arrived in Tuscumbia, he had hoped to have a pontoon bridge laid in short order so that Stewart's and Cheatham's corps could move across the river and join Lee's corps on the north bank at Florence, with the move north beginning in a few days.[12] Almost immediately, however, Hood began to fall behind schedule.

The weather, which had been generally favorable during October, turned foul as November arrived, with cold wind and rain that caused the Tennessee River

General P.G.T. Beauregard, commander, Confederate Military Division of the West. Hood's immediate superior, Beauregard approved the plan for the Tennessee Campaign and organized the logistic support for the Army of Tennessee. *Library of Congress.*

to rise and made life miserable for both man and beast in the Confederate camps. This, of course, complicated the work on the bridge. A few days into the construction, some Federal cavalrymen managed to slip in and cut a section of pontoons loose, and not long after that, the rising river took out another section. Instead of a few days, it took almost two weeks before Frank Cheatham's corps and the supply train were able to cross. Another spell of miserable weather then delayed the rest of the troops for six more days, but by November 20, Hood's army was on the north bank of the Tennessee River.

The only good thing about the delay was that, during the last week, Nathan Bedford Forrest and his troopers began to arrive. Back at Gadsden, General Beauregard had sent orders to Forrest to join Hood in Tennessee, thinking he was in camp at Corinth, Mississippi. In fact, Forrest had taken his men on another raid into west Tennessee. On November 4—the day the Federal cavalrymen cut loose a section of

Hood's pontoon bridge—Forrest and his men were over eighty miles away on the Tennessee River opposite the immense Federal supply base at Johnsonville. That afternoon, Forrest watched as his artillery under Captain John W. Morton sank or disabled several gunboats and steamers at the Johnsonville wharf and then reduced to ashes several million dollars' worth of Northern war materiel awaiting transport to Nashville. Only then did Forrest start back to join Hood at Florence. Because of the cold November rains, the poor roads and the worn-out condition of many of his animals, Forrest's movement from Johnsonville to Florence took two weeks, with his last troops crossing the river on the eighteenth.[13]

When finally assembled on the north bank of the Tennessee River, Hood's infantry numbered about twenty-eight thousand effectives—nine divisions organized into three corps. Brigadier General William "Red" Jackson's cavalry, which had come with Hood from Georgia, combined with Forrest's men and gave Hood an additional mounted force of about five thousand riders, bringing his army up to about thirty-three thousand men of all arms.[14] Over the past three weeks, however, the Federal strength in Middle Tennessee had grown, so Hood's advantage was substantially reduced by November 21. Even so, Hood marched north in a better competitive position than any other major Confederate army in the field at the time.

Hood's opposition at the beginning of the campaign was a hastily assembled force made up of the two infantry corps Major General Sherman had sent back to Tennessee at the end of October. Major General David Stanley and his IV Corps had followed Hood's army as it marched west at the end of October. Moving along the north side of the Tennessee River, they arrived in Athens, Alabama, about the same time Hood arrived at Tuscumbia. When Stanley learned that some of Hood's troops had crossed over to Florence, however, he moved on north to Pulaski, Tennessee, arriving there on about November 4. For the next ten days, Stanley and his men were the only significant Federal infantry between Hood and Nashville. By November 14, elements of the XXIII Corps had arrived at Columbia and Pulaski, and Major General John M. Schofield assumed command of the total force—about twenty-three thousand infantry. Added to the Federal infantry were three cavalry units commanded by Brigadier General John T. Croxton, Brigadier General Edward Hatch and Colonel Horace Capron,[15] bringing Schofield's force up to about twenty-six thousand men.[16]

The command structure of the Federal army at Pulaski was somewhat unusual. David Stanley, commanding the IV Corps, and John Schofield, commanding the XXIII Corps, were both major generals, and both claimed

November 29, 1862, as their date of rank. When their two corps were thrown together to form an army, the question of who would be in overall command naturally came up. Because an issue with the Senate delayed John Schofield's actual confirmation, Stanley considered himself the senior man, but he was only a corps commander. John Schofield's XXIII Corps, although smaller than Stanley's IV Corps, had actually been designated as the Army of the Ohio, so Schofield argued that, as an army commander, he should command. The decision was up to George Thomas in Nashville, and in the end, he sided with Schofield.

On November 21, Hood finally began to move north toward Nashville, with each of his three infantry corps taking a separate route. The weather turned bitterly cold, with snow flurries, but the men made good time, and all three columns were at or near the Tennessee state line by nightfall. To the west, Frank Cheatham's corps moved toward Waynesboro, screened by a small brigade of cavalry led by Colonel Jake Biffle, a native of Wayne County. In the center, S.D. Lee's corps traveled over small country roads toward Henryville, screened by the bulk of James Chalmers's cavalry, with Forrest himself in personal command. Both of these columns were to then turn toward Mount Pleasant, where they would be joined by the third column—A.P. Stewart's corps coming up the main road from Lawrenceburg. From Mount Pleasant, a good turnpike ran northeast about twelve miles to Columbia.

Federal and Confederate cavalry had been skirmishing for several days before the movement north began, and now Forrest stepped up the pressure. By November 23, he had the Federal cavalry on the run. In front of S.D. Lee's column, Forrest, with James Chalmers's command, pushed Horace Capron's outnumbered little brigade steadily back through Henryville. Near Fouche Springs late in the afternoon, Forrest narrowly missed being shot during an engagement but by sundown had pushed Capron back to the outskirts of Mount Pleasant. To the east, "Red" Jackson and Abraham Buford's divisions, screening A.P. Stewart's column, pressed Croxton and Hatch's Federal cavalry all day, driving them out of Lawrenceburg and several miles toward Pulaski. The day had not gone well for the Federal cavalry, and the next day would be more of the same.

As soon as John Schofield got word that the Confederates had begun to move north, he started moving some of his infantry north out of Pulaski, with two of his divisions camped around Lynnville by the night of the twenty-second. By the end of the day on the twenty-third, however, Schofield was in a tight spot. A sizable part of Forrest's cavalry was

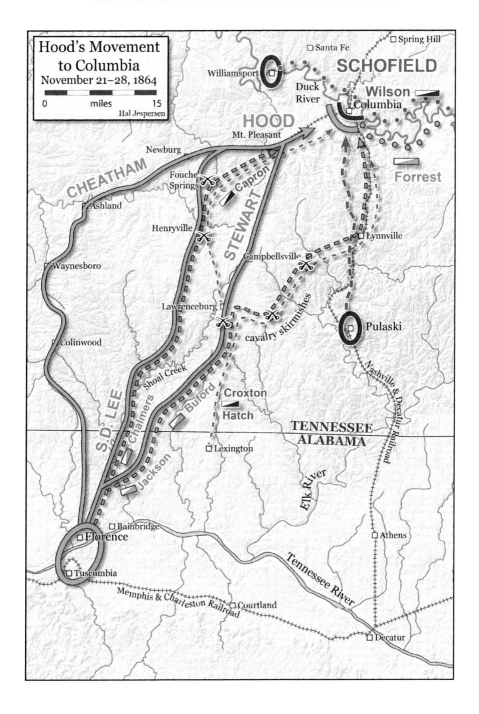

Hood's Movement
to Columbia
November 21–28, 1864

0   miles   15

Hal Jespersen

pressing Capron's brigade at Mount Pleasant and were closer to the vital crossing of the Duck River at Columbia than was Schofield. At the time, Columbia was held by only three regiments of Brigadier General Thomas Ruger's division. In the early hours of November 24, Schofield ordered all his infantry to march to Columbia and secure the river crossing ahead of Forrest's troops. Jacob Cox's division of the XXIII Corps was the closest to Columbia and was on the road before dawn.

Nathan Bedford Forrest had his cavalry up early on the twenty-fourth as well. James Chalmers renewed the fight with Horace Capron's overmatched little brigade and soon had it pushed through the village of Mount Pleasant and in full flight up the pike toward Columbia. One Federal officer described Capron's retreat as more like a stampede. About three miles south of Columbia, however, Horace Capron and his men finally had a bit of good luck. Drawn up across the pike was a line of Federal infantry. Jacob Cox's weary division had been on the road since about 4:00 a.m. The men had marched up the Pulaski Pike and then west on country lanes and had arrived on the Mount Pleasant Pike a few minutes earlier. Capron's men thankfully rode through Cox's line, and the Federal infantry turned back James Chalmers's Confederates after a sharp engagement.

Forrest's other troops under "Red" Jackson and Abraham Buford were also pressing the Federal cavalry east of Lawrenceburg that morning. After skirmishing with John Croxton's troops all day on the twenty-third, Jackson and Buford's men caught up with Edward Hatch's Federal cavalry near the little village of Campbellsville. During a short but intense engagement, the Federals suffered almost two hundred casualties but were able to retire by a side road to Lynnville. From there, Hatch successfully screened the withdrawal of the last of the Federal infantry up the Pulaski Pike and into Columbia. By sundown on November 24, the town and its vital bridges across the Duck River were firmly in Federal hands.

After being delayed for three weeks in northern Alabama, John Bell Hood's invasion of Middle Tennessee had finally begun. In spite of the cold weather and miserable roads, the troops were in generally good spirits and happy to be on the offensive after so many months falling back from the Federal army. The Tennessee regiments were also glad to finally be coming home after over a year in north Georgia. So far, all the fighting had been between the Federal and Confederate cavalry, and Nathan Bedford Forrest had lived up to his reputation, pushing the Northern riders back everywhere. As both armies now settled in around the town of Columbia, Tennessee, however, the infantry would soon get its chance.

Chapter 3

Columbia to Spring Hill

The first four days of the Tennessee Campaign has often been described by historians as a close race for the Duck River at Columbia, with the smaller Federal army in danger of being cut off from its headquarters and support in Nashville. While it is true that John Schofield was anxious to fall back and secure the Duck River crossings ahead of Hood's army, as it turned out, the race wasn't close at all, and Columbia was never in serious danger. Even if Jacob Cox's division had not been able to march to the rescue of Horace Capron's stampeded brigade on the morning of November 24, James Chalmers and his 1,500 or so pursuing Confederate troopers would not have been able to simply ride into Columbia. That morning, the town's Federal garrison numbered almost twice Chalmers's lightly armed cavalry and was dug in behind fortifications, and the closest Confederate infantry forces were still two days away.[17]

All during the morning of the twenty-fourth, David Stanley's IV Corps followed Jacob Cox's division up the pike from Pulaski and into Columbia. After dark, Croxton's brigade and Hatch's division, who had been screening the rear of Stanley's column since their engagement at Campbellsville earlier in the day, came in as well. By the morning of the twenty-fifth, all of Schofield's forces were inside the perimeter at Columbia. All this was observed by Forrest's cavalry, which was in no position to interfere.

It was during the retreat from Pulaski that another Federal senior commander arrived on the scene. James H. Wilson was only four years out of West Point but was already a major general. Wilson had been with McClellan as a topographical engineer during the Peninsular Campaign in 1862 and then transferred to the west to become Grant's inspector general during the Vicksburg Campaign. Earlier in 1864, he had led cavalry under Phil Sheridan in the fighting around Richmond. In the fall of 1864, Wilson was sent back west, and by early November, he was in Nashville, reporting to Major General George Thomas, who put him in charge of all the cavalry in the Military Division of the Mississippi. Wilson immediately began reorganizing his scattered units but soon decided where he was needed most. Ordering all the reinforcements that could be found to push south toward Columbia, Wilson left Nashville by train on November 21, and two days later, he met with Major General Schofield near Lynnville and took personal command of the cavalry in the field.[18]

Once back in Columbia, the Federal cavalry soon crossed to the north side of the Duck River, and Wilson began sorting out and

Major General James H. Wilson, commander of cavalry, Federal Military Division of the Mississippi. Wilson arrived just as the Tennessee Campaign began. He reorganized the various mounted units and commanded the Federal cavalry throughout the campaign and the pursuit during the Confederate retreat from Nashville. *Library of Congress.*

reorganizing his scattered units. Hatch's division, along with Croxton and especially Capron's small brigades, had taken a beating over the last week or so. Two new regiments were added to Capron's brigade, and it, along with Croxton's brigade, was formed into a new division under Brigadier General R.W. Johnson. By the morning of November 28, most of the Federal cavalry was spread along the north side of the Duck River, watching the fords above (east of) Columbia. Nobody believed the Confederates would be idle for long, and they were right. James Wilson was no stranger to cavalry operations, and he did his best to be ready. But he had never met anyone like the man he was about to face.

Major General Nathan Bedford Forrest, cavalry commander, Confederate Army of Tennessee. Forrest's cavalry led the way into Middle Tennessee but was marginalized by Hood at both Franklin and Nashville. Forrest then covered the army's retreat from Columbia to the Tennessee River. *Douglas Bostick.*

In a war filled with interesting and exceptional characters, Nathan Bedford Forrest was in a class all by himself. The son of a poor blacksmith, Forrest had become a millionaire by 1861, speculating in land and cotton and buying and selling slaves in West Tennessee. At age forty, Forrest enlisted as a private soldier along with his brother and fifteen-year-old son, but he was soon commissioned a lieutenant colonel and raised and equipped a mounted unit at his own expense. Riding at the head of the Third Tennessee Cavalry, it soon became apparent that Forrest was a man who had found his calling.

At six feet, two inches, Forrest was a head taller than most of his men and had an intensity in battle that left other men in awe. Major David C. Kelly, a Methodist minister and Forrest's second in command at Fort Donelson, said the following about the first time he saw Forrest in action in Sacramento, Kentucky: "I could scarcely believe him to be the man I had known for several months. His face was flushed and his eyes…were blazing with the intense glare of a panther's, springing upon its prey."[19]

With no military training at all, Forrest turned out to have a natural eye for terrain and a common-sense genius for tactics, unencumbered by a West Point education. Forrest's battles are still studied in military academies today. Add to that a vocabulary of profanity second to none, the personal courage of a lion, the constitution of an ox and a back-street knife fighter's instincts for his opponent's weakness, and you have what the Union army came to call "that Devil Forrest!"

For all his effectiveness against the enemy, however, Forrest could also be a very difficult man to work with or for. He was, at times, almost as much a vexation to his own side as a subordinate as he was to the enemy as an opponent. An eminently confident and practical man, Forrest did not suffer fools of any rank. He once told his own commander that if he ever again interfered with Forrest's troops, it would be "at the peril of your life." Ironically, Forrest himself was almost killed by one of his own junior officers for what the young man perceived to be an insult to his honor.[20]

By the evening of Sunday, November 27, all of Hood's troops had arrived in the vicinity of Columbia, and he called a meeting of his corps commanders at Beechlawn, the home of Major Amos Warfield, which Hood was using as a headquarters. At the meeting, Hood laid out his plan for outflanking Schofield's army and cutting it off from Nashville. The first part of the plan, which was to begin the next morning, was to move the Federal cavalry away from the Duck River crossings east of Columbia and back toward Lewisburg Pike. This was Forrest's job. Once this was done, Hood would move seven infantry divisions across the river on a pontoon bridge, move around the Federal army's left flank and then cut them off at Spring Hill. While this was going on, his two remaining divisions and most of the army's artillery were to move into Columbia, which the enemy was abandoning, and shell the Federals in their new position across the river. The hope was that Schofield would think that most of Hood's army was still in Columbia and would stay in place long enough for Hood to get behind him.

As Hood's staff meeting was going on that Sunday night, the Federal army was indeed on the move. John Schofield had decided that rather than trying to hold the town with the river at his back, he would move across the river and set up his line along a ridge on the north bank. The crossing was completed by the following morning, after which the Federals burned their pontoons and dropped a span of the railroad bridge. The Federal army's evacuation of Columbia saved the town from being destroyed during a battle, but it did not save it from the Confederate army, which contained some the best foragers in the world. No property—public or private—was safe as the Southerners moved in.

Forrest began his part of the operation on the morning of the twenty-eighth with his troops approaching the Duck River at four different places east of Columbia. James Chalmers's division crossed at Holland Ford, near the mouth of Fountain Creek, and moved north, encountering no real resistance. A few miles to the east, Jackson's division crossed unopposed at Wallace's Mill about midday and also moved north. Forrest himself crossed with a small force led by Colonel Jake Biffle. The location is not certain, but it was likely at Davis Ford, where the Confederate engineers went to work preparing the banks for Hood's pontoon bridge. The last of Forrest's troops—Abraham Buford's division—approached the river at Hardison's Mill on the Lewisburg Pike. Here, however, Horace

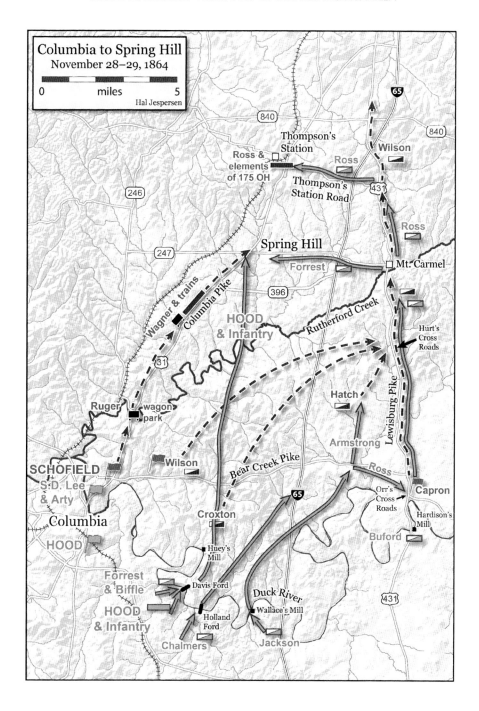

Columbia to Spring Hill
November 28–29, 1864

0   miles   5
Hal Jespersen

Capron's brigade held the north bank and resisted Buford's crossing all that afternoon.

The Federal cavalry did not contest any of the crossings of Forrest's troops except at Hardison's Mill, but they had pickets at all the fords, and by late morning, Major General Wilson knew that Forrest was across the Duck River in strength at several points. Given Forrest's reputation as a raider, Wilson concluded that he was making a run for the Lewisburg Pike, which could then take him directly into Franklin and possibly on to Brentwood and Nashville. By early afternoon, Wilson had issued orders to all his units to fall back and concentrate at Hurt's Crossroads to try to block Forrest. Unfortunately, the orders did not reach Horace Capron, whose brigade continued to resist the Confederate's attempts to cross at Hardison's Mill until almost sundown.

Unlike James Wilson, who grew up in Illinois and had been in the area around Columbia for less than a week, this was Nathan Bedford Forrest's home ground. He had been born a few miles to the east at Chapel Hill and had ridden and raided all over Maury and Williamson Counties the previous year when he was stationed at Spring Hill under the command of Major General Earl Van Dorn. In fact, Forrest was the only senior Confederate commander who had fought over the ground at Spring Hill and Franklin before. Just as he had on the way up from the Tennessee River, Forrest was moving the Federal cavalry just where he wanted it.

All afternoon, Forrest and James Chalmers's division pushed Wilson's Federal cavalry back toward Hurt's Crossroads while Jackson's men moved parallel to them a few miles to the east. Late in the day, as they reached the Shelbyville Road (near present-day Bear Creek Pike), Jackson sent Brigadier General Lawrence Sullivan "Sul" Ross's brigade of Texans to the east while his other brigade, under Brigadier General Frank Armstrong, continued on north toward Hurt's Crossroads. Within a few miles, Ross's lead regiment—the Third Texas—rode into Horace Capron's headquarters area at Orr's Crossroads (the intersection of Lewisburg Pike and present-day Highway 99), setting off quite a skirmish in the twilight. Colonel Capron and his staff, along with most of the Seventh Ohio Cavalry, which had been guarding the ambulances and wagons, were scattered but managed to escape up the road toward Hurt's Crossroads, leaving the other four regiments of the brigade cut off about a mile south at Hardison's Mill, where they had been holding off Abraham Buford's division all afternoon. One of the regiments was the Fifth Iowa, commanded by Major J.M. Young.

In his after-action report, Major Young said that at about 5:00 p.m., his pickets reported "the enemy in force in my rear and Col. Capron, commanding the brigade, gone." In what was probably the bravest action by the Federal cavalry that day, Major Young organized his own Fifth Iowa along with the Fourteenth and Sixteenth Illinois and the Eighth Michigan and, in the approaching darkness, charged straight through Ross's Texans, firing carbines and swinging sabers, and managed to bring his men through to Hurt's Crossroads with little loss.[21]

All day on the twenty-eighth, Forrest had done his job—moving almost all of the Federal cavalry back away from the Duck River fords and clearing the way for Hood's infantry. As Wilson fell back to the Lewisburg Pike, he sent reports to Schofield, still in front of Columbia, that Forrest was across the river in force and that Hood and the infantry were likely close behind. Wilson correctly guessed that Spring Hill would be Hood's objective and strongly suggested that Schofield start falling back on the town before he was cut off. The next morning, he would be proven right.[22]

During the night of November 28–29, the Federal cavalry concentrated at Hurt's Crossroads while Forrest moved up near it with all his troops except Buford's division, which was still several miles south at Hardison's Mill and would join him before noon on the twenty-ninth. The morning of the twenty-ninth started out badly for James Wilson and his men as Forrest soon flanked them out of their position and sent them retreating up Lewisburg Pike toward the little community of Mount Carmel. By 10:00 a.m., the last of the Federal rear guard—Colonel John Croxton's brigade—had fallen back to Mount Carmel, closely pressed by Frank Armstrong's Confederates. At Mount Carmel, however, Armstrong found Colonel Datus E. Coon's brigade, dismounted and posted behind barricades. Croxton's men passed through the Federal line, and Coon's men turned back two charges by Armstrong's riders.

Even so, the Federals didn't stay long at Mount Carmel. More than ever convinced that Forrest was aiming for Franklin or Nashville, James Wilson soon had his men falling back up Lewisburg Pike to block such a move, which was exactly what Forrest wanted. He left "Sul" Ross's Texas brigade—about six hundred men—to push Wilson farther north up the pike and turned the rest of his troops (over four thousand men) west on what is today Duplex Road. It was just before 11:00 a.m., and the little town of Spring Hill, with its vital road junction, was five miles away.

Meanwhile, John Schofield had spent November 28 outside Columbia with his infantry on a ridge overlooking the Duck River. Some lively skirmishing had gone on as the Confederates moved into town and began to make contact with the Federal infantry guarding the fords. By early afternoon, however, reports had come in from Major General Wilson's headquarters of Confederate cavalry crossing the river in force east of Columbia, and Wilson had said that he was moving northeast to the Lewisburg Pike. By 2:00 p.m., Schofield had agreed to the cavalry's move, but while the cavalry fought to the east along Lewisburg Pike, he spent the rest of the day with little new information since Forrest's movements cut off his communication with Wilson.

In the early hours of November 29, James Wilson was finally able to send a dispatch to Schofield, giving a brief report of the action of the twenty-eighth and advising Schofield to fall back with the infantry as far as Franklin. By 8:15 a.m. on the twenty-ninth, Schofield had replied to Wilson's dispatch and was getting some—but not all—of his army in motion.[23] Major General David Stanley, commanding the IV Corps, was ordered to start the wagon train and the reserve artillery back north on the Franklin Pike to Spring Hill and escort it with two of his divisions—Wagner's and Kimball's. Not long after Stanley set off with the wagons, however, reports came in of Confederate infantry moving around the left flank of Schofield's position.[24] In case the enemy was planning to attack the current Federal position at Columbia, Kimball's division was ordered to stop a few miles up the pike at Rutherford Creek while Stanley continued with Wagner's division and the supply train on to Spring Hill.

The reports of Confederate infantry crossing the river east of Columbia were true. This was the second part of John Bell Hood's plan. As soon as Forrest moved the Federal cavalry back on the twenty-eighth, Hood's engineers had gone to work at Davis Ford, preparing the approaches and laying a pontoon bridge. The infantry moved into position during the night, and at first light on that Tuesday morning, Frank Cheatham's corps, with Patrick Cleburne's division in the lead, began crossing the river. By 9:00 a.m., they had been followed by A.P. Stewart's corps and Ed Johnson's division of S.D. Lee's corps. The rest of Hood's army—S.D. Lee's two remaining divisions and most of the artillery—was still in Columbia. Lee's job was to shell the Federals across the river all day in the hope that Schofield would believe the Confederates' main force was still in the town. By mid-morning, however, the Federal commander knew he was being flanked to the east. He already had his wagon train on the road, thanks to James Wilson's warning. Unsure of the Confederate infantry's objective, however, John Schofield chose to keep the rest of his army at Columbia for several more hours, and this decision almost cost him his army.

By about 11:00 a.m. on November 29, three columns were converging on the vital crossroads at the small village of Spring Hill. From the east, along the Mount Carmel road, came Nathan Bedford Forrest and at least four thousand cavalry. From Columbia on the Franklin Pike came David Stanley, escorting eight hundred wagons and the Federal army's reserve artillery with about five thousand men of George Wagner's division. Finally, marching up from the Duck River came John Bell Hood at the head of at least twenty thousand Confederate infantry. Before the day was over, they would all meet and play their parts in one of the biggest missed opportunities of the Civil War.

Chapter 4

The Affair at Spring Hill

The town of Spring Hill, Tennessee, sits on Columbia Pike (today's Highway 31) almost halfway between the larger towns of Franklin and Columbia, and by November 1864, the town had already seen a good deal of the war. During the spring and early summer of 1863, Spring Hill had been the headquarters of a Confederate cavalry corps commanded by Major General Earl Van Dorn while the Federals occupied Franklin, twelve miles to the north. In early March, the two forces met at Thompson Station, where the Confederates under Van Dorn and Nathan Bedford Forrest captured the better part of a Federal brigade. During his stay in Spring Hill, Major General Van Dorn had his headquarters in the home of Martin Cheairs. Unfortunately, when he was not conducting military operations, Van Dorn was accused of paying inappropriate attention to Jessie McKissack Peters, the pretty young wife of a local doctor who was away from home at the time. On returning home, Jessie's husband took exception to the rumors, and on May 7, 1863, Dr. James B. Peters entered Van Dorn's office and shot the general in the head, leaving Forrest in command.[25]

By early July 1863, the Confederates were driven out of Middle Tennessee, and the Federals had occupied Spring Hill for the last sixteen months. On the morning of November 29, the town was defended by about two hundred troops—a detachment of the Twelfth Tennessee Cavalry (U.S.) under the command of Lieutenant Colonel Charles C. Hoefling. Their job was to picket the surrounding roads and run a dispatch line between army headquarters at Columbia and the nearest telegraph station at Franklin—a distance of about twenty-two miles. By the middle of the morning, however, Hoefling began to receive some unexpected but very welcome reinforcements.

The day before, when it became certain that Forrest was crossing the Duck River east of Columbia, Brigadier General Edward Hatch had ordered some small units that had been sent to guard river crossings west of town to withdraw. So it was that parts of two cavalry regiments rode into Spring Hill that morning in search of Hatch's division, which was out of contact several miles to the east. Hoefling was overjoyed to have them since he had just received word that some of his pickets east of Spring Hill had been driven in by a large force of Confederate cavalry moving to attack the approaching wagon train. Forrest was coming. About this time, Company M of the Second Michigan Cavalry also wandered in, having been cut off from Croxton's command during the fighting the day before. It was pressed into service as well, and shortly after 11:00 a.m., the cobbled-together defense force of fewer than a thousand men rode out to meet Forrest and at least four thousand Confederates.[26]

About two miles east of town, the Federal defenders went into position on the Mount Carmel road just before the Confederates skirmishers arrived. When his advanced units began to run into opposition, Forrest brought up Frank Armstrong's brigade and a couple other units and ordered a charge. Hoefling's men had a good position along the crest of a hill, however, and turned back Forrest's initial attack.[27] Their success, however, was only temporary, and they knew it. Outnumbered as they were, all they could hope to do was buy time until help could arrive. Before riding out, Hoefling had sent a courier down the pike to warn the wagon train he knew was approaching and urge it to hurry. His message reached Major General David Stanley when he was still two miles away. Hoefling's little force was doing its best, but he and his men were overmatched. The arrival of the Federal infantry was the only thing that could save the town from Forrest's cavalry.

Ranging ahead of the wagon train were four companies of the Seventy-third Illinois. They were the first Federal infantry to reach Spring Hill and engage Forrest's troops as they pushed Hoefling's defenders back into town around noon. Within a few minutes, the rest of Colonel Emerson Opdycke's brigade arrived on the run, followed by John Q. Lane's brigade, and Forrest had lost his chance. It had now been thirty-six hours since the Confederates had crossed the Duck River. Both the men and the horses were exhausted, and more importantly, many of Forrest's units were down to their last few cartridges. He simply didn't have the power to take the town now that the Federal infantry had arrived.

That afternoon, a few miles to the north, the last of Forrest's troops were also in action. Brigadier General "Sul" Ross and his brigade broke contact with the Federal cavalry pushing toward Franklin on the Lewisburg Pike and turned west on the Thompson Station Road. A few miles later, at the intersection with the Columbia Pike, they had run into a detachment of the 175th Ohio, moving wagons and prisoners toward Franklin. Ross and his men scattered the Ohio troops, captured a wagon and intercepted a train coming into the Thompson Station depot. Ross and his men eventually forced the evacuation of the depot as well, but toward evening, they withdrew to the east and settled in to watch the pike from the hills near the road.[28]

By early afternoon, two of the columns converging on Spring Hill had arrived, with David Stanley and the Federals winning the first round. They now had over six thousand men holding the town, strongly supported by the army's reserve artillery. Things were far from decided, however. Hood was on the way, and his column was the strongest of all. Ten miles to the south at Columbia, John Schofield waited with the bulk of the Federal army, still not sure what his old West Point classmate was up to (Schofield and Hood had both graduated in the class of 1853).

Early that morning, General Hood had gotten all seven divisions of his flanking force across the river without incident or opposition, but the march up to Spring Hill was proving to be slower than he hoped. The straight line distance from Davis Ford, where the infantry crossed, to Spring Hill was about twelve miles. As Hood quickly found out from a local guide, however, the trip along the twisting and narrow country lanes would add at least five miles to the distance. Even worse, moving so many troops would force many of the men off the roads and into the fields. One Alabama soldier later wrote, "Whether on bottom or hills, we sank at every step in mud over our shoes."[29] Even with the extra hardship, however, by 3:00 p.m., Hood's leading division was coming on to Rally Hill Pike (which ran approximately along present-day Kedron Road) near its crossing of Rutherford Creek.

So far, Hood's plan to outflank Schofield's Federal army and cut off its retreat to Nashville had worked very well. Forrest had moved almost all the Federal cavalry off to the northeast and completely out of the fight. Although exhausting, Hood's march from the Duck River with his infantry had been unopposed. S.D. Lee's artillery bombardment of the Federal position at Columbia was continuing and could be heard by the Confederates as they approached Spring Hill. Unknown to Hood, Schofield had just now (about

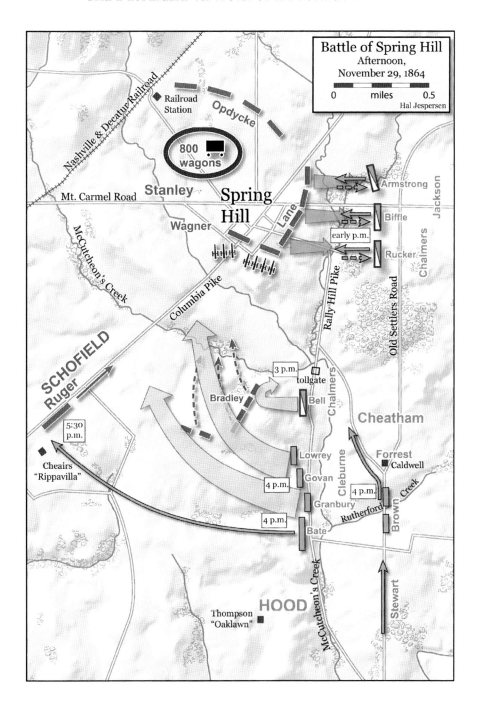

3:00 p.m.) begun to move the rest of his army back from Columbia, but they had a ten-mile march in front of them. Hood had about two hours of daylight left and would shortly have almost ten thousand men within a mile or so of the town, with another ten thousand or more close behind. With the Federal garrison of about six thousand men committed to protecting the town and the vital wagon train parked near the railroad depot, there was no way they could deny Hood possession of the pike south of Spring Hill if his troops could get there. The events that transpired over the next few hours would be debated by the men who were there for the rest of their lives and have been researched by historians for the last 150 years. What happened is pretty well known. Why it happened is still disputed even today.

Shortly after 3:00 p.m., Major General Patrick Cleburne's division, leading Frank Cheatham's corps and Hood's whole force, reached Rutherford Creek, and the men took off their shoes and begin to wade across. Within a few minutes, they were marching up Rally Hill Pike, accompanied by Hood and their corps commander, Major General Frank Cheatham. About a mile from Rutherford Creek, General Hood ordered Cleburne's men to halt and move off the road to their left, facing to the west.[30] About a mile in front of them, across open fields, was the Columbia Pike, and to their right were some low, wooded hills. Cleburne's orders, given by Hood, were to block the pike and then face toward Columbia.[31] It was almost 4:00 p.m. by the time Cleburne's division was formed and stepped off. The prime objective of Hood's plan was just one mile away.

When Brigadier General George Wagner's division hurried into town around noontime, it was Colonel Emerson Opdycke's brigade that arrived first and went into position covering the north side of town and the wagon park. Next came Colonel John Q. Lane's brigade, which extended the line around the east side of town and back to the pike near the Martin Cheairs home. Wagner's last brigade to arrive—at about 2:00 p.m.—was commanded by Brigadier General Luther Bradley, and instead of going into line with the other troops, Bradley's brigade was pushed out to the southeast about one thousand yards and went into position on a wooded knoll that overlooked the Rally Hill Pike.

From their advanced position, Bradley's men were not in contact with the rest of the Federal line, but they had an excellent view of the most likely avenue of approach of the Confederate infantry, which the Federal command in Spring Hill knew was coming. Shortly after Bradley's men arrived, Forrest sent in some men from Tyree Bell's brigade to probe the position and found the Sixty-fourth Ohio, which had been sent out to skirmish. After a brief engagement, both Forrest's men and the Ohio regiment fell back without the Confederates discovering the extent of the Federal position, and Bradley's men continued to dig in along the tree line. As a result, when Cleburne started his division across the field to take the pike almost an hour later, he did not know that he would be marching past six enemy regiments, dug in along his right flank.[32]

Cleburne's division formed up with Brigadier General Mark Lowery's brigade on the right and Brigadier General Hiram Granbury's on the left in echelon (set back slightly). In the center and to the rear, Cleburne rode with Brigadier General Daniel Govan's brigade, which was his reserve. Forrest ordered Bell's cavalry to screen Cleburne's right, but with only four rounds of ammunition per man remaining, Bell knew he would be of little use. At about 4:15 p.m.—after it had moved about halfway to the pike—Lowery's right passed within one hundred yards of Bradley's line, and two of the Federal regiments opened fire. Lowery's men were veterans, and he soon had them turned to face the new threat. Within a few minutes, Cleburne had turned Govan's reserve brigade as well and brought it up on Lowery's right, and Luther Bradley's brigade was soon in trouble. Seeing the Confederates moving around his right flank, Bradley rode in that direction but was seriously wounded before he could rally his men.

Cleburne's last brigade, under Hiram Granbury, continued toward the pike for some distance after the rest of the division turned north. They routed the Thirty-sixth Illinois that was supporting a section of Pennsylvania artillery and sent the infantry and the guns retreating back toward town, but they stopped short of the road.

Soon after Bradley was wounded, the Federal line began to come apart, and the men fell back toward the town and the relative safety of the main Federal line, closely pursued by Lowery and Govan's Confederates. The Federals fell back through the timber and across a couple of small streams to the high ground just behind the Martin Cheairs home, where David Stanley has stationed at least two batteries of artillery. Most of Bradley's men scrambled past the guns, and Stanley's artillery turned back the Confederates, even wounding Cleburne's favorite horse, Red Pepper.[33]

Even though Luther Bradley's brigade could not hold its advanced position long, it still performed what turned out to be an invaluable service by drawing Cleburne's attention away from the pike, which was his primary objective. Bradley's attack caused Cleburne to turn his entire division almost ninety degrees—from west to north—so that, although Granbury's brigade came close, none of his units reached the road.[34] There was still some daylight left, however, and there were still other chances.

Following Cleburne up Rally Hill Pike was Major General William B. Bate's division. As Cleburne was stepping off, Bate was just leaving the pike and forming up some distance to the south. Bate had been told by Cheatham, his corps commander, to support Cleburne on the left, but Cleburne had already moved out of sight when General Hood himself came by and told Bate to simply march west to the pike and then face toward Columbia. Having been ordered by the commanding general himself, Bate stepped off just after 4:00 p.m.[35] His division numbered about two thousand men, and they were almost a mile and three quarters from the pike. Not long after he started across the fields, Bate heard firing off to his right and knew that Cleburne had become engaged, but his view of the action was blocked by some high ground. Bate continued on toward the pike, angling to his right and hoping that he could eventually link up with Cleburne's left once he got there. All during Cleburne's fight with Bradley's brigade, Bate marched on toward the pike—out of sight and out of contact—half a mile to the south.

Unaware that Cleburne had swung his division around to the north, Bate approached the Columbia Pike in the twilight, just after 5:00 p.m. Instead of finding the left flank of Cleburne's division, however, Bate's skirmishers collided with about one hundred men of the Twenty-sixth Ohio who had been left to guard a small side road. The Confederates quickly scattered the tiny Ohio regiment but then realized that more Federal troops were approaching. It was Silas Strickland's brigade—the advance unit of Brigadier General Thomas Ruger's division that was leading the rest of the Federal army up from Columbia. Riding along with Ruger was John Schofield. As his skirmishers engaged the head of the Federal column, William Bate formed up his division and prepared to lead his men to block the pike. They were about three hundred yards away, just north of Rippaville, the home of Martin Cheairs's brother Nathaniel. Just as Bate was preparing to move, however, a courier rode up with a message that changed everything.

Benjamin Franklin Cheatham had been commanding men since the war began. Although not a professional soldier, he had served in the Mexican-American War and risen to the rank of colonel. After a stint in California during the gold rush, Cheatham came back to Tennessee to run the family plantation. He also served in the state militia until the war began and was then commissioned a Confederate brigadier general. By the Battle of Shiloh, Cheatham was a major general, and after Atlanta, he had been given command of William Hardee's old corps. On this particular afternoon, he was trying to get his three divisions organized for an attack on the town of Spring Hill. Unfortunately, it seems that Cheatham and his commander, General Hood, had fundamentally different ideas as to the objective that day. Hood, from the orders he gave to both Cleburne and Bate, indicated that the first priority was to block the pike directly in front of them and south of town. Cheatham, however, was intent on attacking the town itself and wanted all three of his divisions in place for a coordinated effort.

Once Cleburne began his advance, Cheatham started back toward Rutherford Creek to bring up his next division. General Hood, however, had already ordered that division (Bate) to march west to the pike

Major General Benjamin F. Cheatham, corps commander, Confederate Army of Tennessee. Cheatham was given command of Hardee's corps after Atlanta. His three divisions fought at Spring Hill, attacked the Federal center at Franklin and were then practically destroyed at Nashville. *Library of Congress.*

without Cheatham's knowledge. Not finding Bate but assuming that he was somewhere to Cleburne's left, Cheatham moved on to his last division, commanded by Major General John C. Brown, and ordered it to move up into position on Cleburne's right. It was not until he was moving Brown into position opposite the Federal line held by Lane's brigade east of the town that Cheatham learned that Cleburne had driven Bradley's brigade back and was now preparing to assault the Federal position near the Martin Cheairs House on his own. Wanting a combined effort for the push on the town, Cheatham ordered Cleburne to hold his position until Brown could get in position and initiate the attack. The sound of Brown's guns would be Cleburne's signal to advance. Since it was almost 5:00 p.m. and rapidly getting dark, Brown was told to advance without delay.

Having given his orders to Brown and Cleburne, Frank Cheatham and some of his staff rode off to the southwest in search of Bate's division, which was still out of contact with the rest of the corps. Before he had gone far, however, Cheatham began to wonder why he had not heard gunfire from Brown's direction since he should have already been in contact with the enemy. Cheatham then decided to send a courier on to find Bate, while Cheatham himself would return to Brown to see what had gone wrong. On arriving, Cheatham found that Brown had advanced about four hundred yards when enemy soldiers appeared on his unsupported right flank, which he thought was being covered by Forrest's cavalry. Seeing what he thought were enemy soldiers in a position to attack his exposed right and rear, Brown halted his entire division. He later said that he felt "in a position where I must meet with inevitable disaster if I advanced on Spring Hill."[36]

Since Brown had not yet opened fire, half a mile or so to Brown's left, a very frustrated Patrick Cleburne was required, by Cheatham's orders, to remain in position. Cleburne's men maintained, from that day on, that if they had been allowed to attack, they could have captured the town in short order. According to an aide, it was a "bitter disappointment" to Cleburne to be ordered to delay his attack. Since he was killed the next day at Franklin, Cleburne left no record of his thoughts on the matter. However, Daniel Govan, one of his brigade commanders and one of the last people to see Cleburne alive, had no doubt that "had we not been halted…we could in 20 minutes have captured or destroyed Stanley together with 800 wagons and his artillery, and have planted our army firmly on the pike."[37]

About this time, Frank Cheatham arrived and conferred with Brown. There are different versions of what was or was not said, but all agree that upon personally viewing Brown's position, Cheatham and some others rode back to headquarters to confer with General Hood.[38] It was while Cheatham was on his way to Hood's headquarters that his courier finally reached William Bate with orders for him to move to his right and link up with Cleburne's left. This presented Bate with quite a dilemma. This new order from his corps commander contradicted the orders Bate had received directly from the army commander, and the pike was only a few hundred yards in front of him. Unwilling to give up his position, Bate sent his own courier back to find Cheatham and confirm the order. Bate's staff officer eventually found his corps commander at headquarters with General Hood. Cheatham, still concerned with bringing all three of his divisions into contact and unaware of the opportunity that lay in front of Bate, had no time to deal with troublesome subordinates. He told the courier that Bate had a choice—he could either obey the order immediately or report to headquarters under arrest. On confirmation of the direct order, Bate

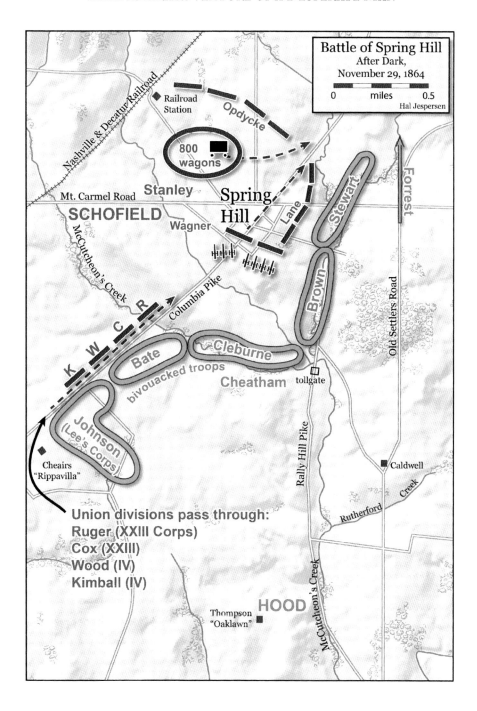

Battle of Spring Hill
After Dark,
November 29, 1864

0   miles   0.5

Hal Jespersen

reluctantly pulled back from the pike and began to move to his right through the darkness—and the Confederate's last chance to block the pike before dark was lost.

John Bell Hood would continue on through the night trying to find some way to block the pike either south or north of Spring Hill. Even with the failure to capture the road before sundown, Hood believed that the bulk of the Federal army would still be within reach the next morning and that the enemy might even decide to surrender.[39] In fact, the fight was already over. Patrick Cleburne's short engagement with Luther Bradley's brigade would be the only significant combat at Spring Hill.

Chapter 5

The Federal Retreat to Franklin

It was almost full dark that Tuesday evening when the resistance Thomas Ruger's lead brigade had encountered on Columbia Pike just north Rippaville suddenly tapered off and then ceased altogether. John Schofield, riding along with Ruger, had no way of knowing that the enemy (Bate's division) had been ordered to fall back, but he lost no time in moving his column on toward Spring Hill. They passed close enough to the men of Patrick Cleburne and William Bate's divisions on the east side of the road to see men around campfires and hear some of them talking but arrived safely in Spring Hill at about 7:00 p.m. There were three more Federal divisions to come, but they had been ordered not to leave the Duck River until sundown. It would be almost four hours before the next division arrived. In the meantime, if the Confederates decided to make a night attack, Spring Hill was still terribly vulnerable. It was going be a long and anxious night for the Federal troops.

When Schofield arrived at David Stanley's headquarters, he learned of the Confederate raid on the crossroads and depot at Thompson Station earlier in the day and the fact that Stanley's pickets had recently seen movement of more enemy troops in that direction. After meeting with Stanley, Schofield decided to take Ruger's troops on north to the crossroads at Thompson Station to hold open the army's escape route to Franklin. The march was just over three miles, and when Schofield and Ruger arrived, they found old campfires but no enemy troops.[40] The Confederates (Ross's brigade of cavalry) had fallen back to the hills east of the pike. Schofield left Ruger at the crossroads; sent Captain Twining, his chief engineer, riding on to Franklin at a gallop with dispatches for Nashville; and then returned to Spring Hill.[41]

Even though it was now dark and the rest of the Federal army was beginning to arrive from Columbia, John Bell Hood had not given up on his plan. In fact, over half his troops were still waiting to be sent forward. Lieutenant General A.P. Stewart had followed Cheatham's corps with three divisions of his own plus a division from S.D. Lee's corps. While Cheatham's men tried without success to take the pike south of town, Stewart, on Hood's orders, sat at Rutherford Creek, over a mile away. Sometime after dark, learning that the pike was still open, Hood turned to Stewart and asked him to take his men around the east side of Spring Hill and block the pike north of town. With a local man as a guide, Stewart started out about the same time Schofield and Ruger's men were arriving in Spring Hill.

An hour or two later, Stewart's column was overtaken by a staff officer who said he had been sent by Hood to show him his position. Stewart thought he already understood where his position should be, but after some discussion, he decided to follow this new officer. Before long, however, he realized that they were actually being led farther from the pike, contrary to the orders he had received directly from Hood. To Stewart, this meant that either a mistake had been made or that Hood had changed his mind about what he wanted done. Having his men fall out and rest, Stewart, the staff officer and General Forrest, whose headquarters was nearby, rode back to confirm Stewart's orders with Hood.

It was about 11:00 p.m. by the time Stewart's group reached Hood's headquarters. Stewart told his commander that he was still some distance from the pike and had put his men in bivouac until he could resolve the conflict in his orders. According to Stewart's official report, General Hood agreed that he should allow his men, who had been on the road since sunup, to rest and start again at first light.[42]

After learning of Stewart's situation, Hood turned to Forrest, who had ridden to the meeting with Stewart, and asked if he could put some of his men across the pike north of town. Forrest agreed to try but said that most of his troops were out of ammunition. The only cavalry that Forrest had near the road—and one of the few with any ammunition left—was Jackson's division, of which Ross's brigade near Thompson Station was a part. They had been across the pike earlier, but with fewer than seven hundred men, Ross would be no match for Ruger's infantry, who, unknown to Hood and Forrest, now held the crossroads. Forrest sent off orders to Jackson and tried to find more men and ammunition, but it would be too little and too late.

Brigadier General Jacob Cox was John Schofield's senior division commander, and he had been left to hold the crossings of the Duck River at Columbia until sundown and then lead the other two division of Schofield's army back to Spring Hill. It was almost 6:00 p.m. when Cox's men began to pull out of their position near the river and march north up the pike, followed soon after by T.J. Wood's division. Pickets were left at the river until about midnight to discourage the Confederates from crossing. After being delayed for some time at Rutherford Creek, Cox's column arrived in Spring Hill at about 11:00 p.m. They had moved as quietly as possible past the hundreds of Confederate campfires filling the fields to the right of the pike. So close were the two forces that occasionally a Federal soldier would wander off the road and into a Confederate camp, or a Confederate picket would be captured by a Federal unit.

Once in Spring Hill, Cox conferred with David Stanley and John Schofield, who had just returned from Thompson Station, and it was quickly decided that the army must leave while it had the chance. Cox would move his division on out of town and take the lead up the pike to Franklin, while Ruger's men would fall in behind Cox as he passed Thompson Station. Thomas J. Wood, whose division was next in line, followed Cox through town and then took up a defensive position on the east side of the road between Spring Hill and Thompson Station. Once that was done, the wagon train began to move out of town at about 1:00 a.m., escorted by Nathan Kimball's division, which had been stationed at Rutherford Creek most of the day and was the last to arrive from Columbia. As the train passed, Wood's men were to abandon their defensive position and follow the column on to Franklin.

Shortly after 2:00 a.m., while the Federal wagon train was passing Thompson Station, Forrest's cavalry made the last Confederate effort of the day. Coming down from the hills in the dark, Brigadier General Lawrence Sullivan "Sul" Ross's small brigade hit the Federal wagons near the crossroads. Ross claims that he held the pike for half an hour, destroyed a number of wagons and made off with several teams of horses and mules before being driven back into the hills by Federal infantry.[43] Ross's attack was only a temporary setback, however. Before long, some of Kimball's men restored order and got the train moving again.

By about 5:00 a.m. on November 30, all the pickets from the Duck River had arrived, and the last of the eight hundred Federal wagons were pulling out of town. At about this same time, Jacob Cox's division, at the head of the column, arrived on the south edge of Franklin. The retreating Federal column was now twelve miles long, filling Columbia Pike from Spring Hill

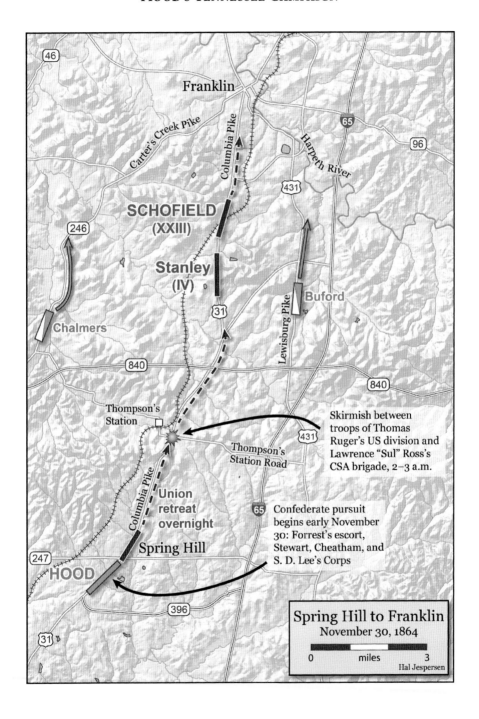

Skirmish between troops of Thomas Ruger's US division and Lawrence "Sul" Ross's CSA brigade, 2–3 a.m.

Confederate pursuit begins early November 30: Forrest's escort, Stewart, Cheatham, and S. D. Lee's Corps

Spring Hill to Franklin
November 30, 1864

0 miles 3

Hal Jespersen

to Franklin. Finally, just about daybreak, George Wagner's division, which had fought the battle and held the town all through the day and night, began to pull back, acting as the army's rear guard. Colonel Emerson Opdycke's brigade, the first one into town, became the last Federal troops to leave, at about 6:00 a.m. Thanks to a tenacious defense led by Major General David Stanley, a good deal of confusion within the Confederate command and a lot of luck, Schofield's army had avoided a disaster. After the war, there would be bitter arguments among the Confederate commanders about who was to blame for this tremendous missed opportunity. Some years later, amid all the controversy, one of Forrest's former officers summed it up as well as anyone: "This whole thing was a wretched affair; let the fault be wherever it may."[44]

Around sunup on November 30, the last of the Federal troops moved out of Spring Hill, and the Confederates began stirring. From their camps alongside the Columbia Pike, it didn't take long for them to realize that something was wrong. From the men in the field to the officers at headquarters, the news ran through the army that the Yankees had gone. Through most of the night, John Bell Hood had continued to believe that some of his units would manage to block the road, so the news took him by surprise. Gathering some of his staff, Hood left Oaklawn, Absalom Thompson's home, and rode west across the fields to Rippavilla on the Columbia Pike, sending couriers out to call some of his officers to a breakfast meeting. Nobody knows for sure who was at the breakfast meeting or what was said, except that General Hood was furious, and according to Susan Cheairs, the lady of the house, the general's language was not fit for women or children.[45]

Meanwhile, some of the Confederate units were already moving to pursue the Federals. Nathan Bedford Forrest, as usual, was up early. Having had to leave all his own ordnance wagons at Columbia, he was finally able to resupply his troops with ammunition from some infantry units and get his men on the road early. He sent James Chalmers's division across to the Carter's Creek Pike to screen the army on the west, as well as one of Abraham Buford's brigades (Crossland's) over to the Lewisburg Pike to do the same on the east. Taking his escort and Tyree Bell's brigade, Forrest then started up the pike in pursuit of the Federal column, picking up units of Jackson's division as he went. Behind him, A.P. Stewart's corps began forming up on the pike.

Whatever was said at the breakfast meeting at Rippavilla was brief. All over the fields south and east of Spring Hill, the Confederates were moving to pursue the Federal army. Stewart's corps was soon on the road with

Cheatham's corps forming up to follow. Finally, S.D. Lee was bringing the rest of the army up from Columbia—Henry Clayton's division in the lead with Carter L. Stevenson's division bringing up the rear with the bulk of the army's artillery. Once they arrived, Major General Ed Johnson's division, which had marched to Spring Hill with Hood the day before but had seen no action, would be reunited with Lee's corps, which would then follow the rest of the army up the road to Franklin as it was able. By sunrise on November 30, the pike, from just north of Columbia through Spring Hill and on to Franklin, was completely taken over by the two armies and would stay that way most of the day.

At any given time that Wednesday, something was happening all along the pike for over twenty miles. By about 8:00 a.m.—from south to north along the road—the rear of S.D. Lee's corps was crossing Rutherford Creek, while his advance units were still an hour from Spring Hill. General Hood's breakfast meeting at Rippaville was breaking up. Frank Cheatham's corps was beginning to march out of town, following A.P. Stewart's men. About two miles north of Thompson Station, near the West Harpeth River, Nathan Bedford Forrest had caught up with the Federal column and was beginning to make hit-and-run attacks on Opdycke's brigade and a section of artillery that was acting as the Federal rear guard—a deadly dance that would continue for the next four hours. Finally, five miles farther north, Brigadier General Jacob Cox's division was hard at work building a defensive line on the southern edge of Franklin while the Federal engineers were a mile farther into town, working desperately on bridges to get the army over the Harpeth River.

The Affair at Spring Hill was over, for better or worse, and the armies were moving north. John Schofield, the Federal commander, was desperately looking for a way to put his army beyond the reach of his old West Point classmate and his dreaded cavalry under Forrest. John Bell Hood, after the devastating failure at Spring Hill, was hoping for one last chance to destroy the Federal army before it could reach the safety of the fortifications at Nashville. As it would happen, the little village of Franklin would provide both men with the opportunity they were seeking—with tragic consequences.

Chapter 6

Franklin—November 30

THE FEDERAL POSITION

Just before 5:00 a.m., Brigadier General Jacob Cox's division, at the head of the Federal column, arrived at the southern edge of the town of Franklin. Riding along with Cox was Major General John Schofield, who ordered him to have his men fall out and have breakfast while the rest of the Federal column passed by. Cox moved his men off the road and then went to a large brick house near the pike. After waking the owner, Cox and his staff began to set up a field headquarters in the family's parlor. The house was the home of Fountain Branch Carter, who had most of his family living there with him—six other adults and his nine grandchildren. Across the road, about 175 yards from the house, sat a large building that housed the Carter family's cotton gin. Since General Cox believed that the army's stay would be brief, the Carter family was allowed to remain on the property and in the part of the house not being used by him and his staff. Soon after moving into Carter's parlor, Cox and his officers stretched out on the carpet and tried to get a little rest for the first time in twenty-four hours.[46]

While Jacob Cox was moving into the Carter House, John Schofield rode on into town in search of his engineering officer, Captain William Twining. Captain Twining had been sent on ahead to open telegraph communications with headquarters in Nashville and to assess the facilities for crossing the army over the Harpeth River. Word had come several days ago that the wagon bridge at Franklin was down, so Schofield had already sent a request

The Carter House and yard as seen from the south, circa 1900. During the battle, sixteen members of the Carter family plus several neighbors and family servants hid in the basement of the main house. Intense hand-to-hand fighting occurred in the yard and around the main house and outbuildings, all of which still bear many bullet marks. *Battle of Franklin Trust, Carter House collection.*

to Nashville for pontoons to replace it, and he hoped to find them waiting at the depot. Unfortunately, Twining, who had been in town since before midnight, had bad news for his commander. The pontoons that would have allowed them to quickly lay a temporary bridge had not arrived.[47]

Without the pontoons, the Federal army was left with only two ways to cross the Harpeth River at Franklin. A few hundred yards from the depot, the Nashville & Decatur Railroad Bridge crossed the river near Fort Granger, which sat on a bluff on the north bank. Farther downstream, near the site of the original turnpike bridge, was a ford that was barely usable since the river had risen from the recent rains. Wagons could still cross at the ford, but it was a slow process. In between the ford and the railroad bridge was what remained of the County Bridge, which had been partially burned a few months earlier. Having no pontoons to replace it, Schofield now ordered that the damaged bridge be repaired so that at least men could cross and that the railroad bridge be planked over to accommodate wagons as well as troops. The army's eight hundred heavy supply wagons, which were now rolling into town and parking along the streets, were the critical element. Until they could be moved across the river, the town and the vital bridges must be held. Schofield now rode back to the Carter House to arrange for that to be done.

Brigadier General Cox and his staff were asleep on Mr. Carter's fine parlor carpet when John Schofield returned from the river. Soon everybody was awake, and the army commander explained the situation. Thirty-three years later, Cox still remembered:

> In all my intimate acquaintance with him, I never saw him so manifestly disturbed by the situation he was in…that morning. Pale and jaded from the long strain of the forty-eight hours just past, he spoke with a deep earnestness of feeling he rarely showed. "General," he said, "the pontoons are not here, the county bridge is gone, and the ford is hardly passable. You must take command of the 23rd Corps and put it in position here to hold Hood back at all hazards till we can get our trains over and fight with the river in front of us. With Twining's help I shall see what can be done to improve the means of crossing, for everything depends on it."[48]

So began what was probably Jacob Cox's finest day in a Federal uniform.

Jacob Dolson Cox was not a West Pointer. He was a lawyer and politician and a graduate of Oberlin College who owed his brigadier general's commission to political connections in Ohio, including fellow state legislator and future president James A. Garfield. Cox, however, was an intelligent man and a good student, and three and a half years of war had turned him into a skilled and dependable soldier. Had it not been for a technicality in Congress, he would have ranked with Schofield as a major general. Cox had commanded a division all through the Atlanta Campaign, so John Schofield felt confident in putting him in charge of the defenses at Franklin.

As soon as the men had finished breakfast, Cox put them to work carrying out General Schofield's orders. Since he had temporarily been elevated to command of the XXIII Corps, Brigadier General James Reilly assumed command of the division and placed the three brigades in position from the banks of the Harpeth River to the Columbia Pike. On the left, between the river and Lewisburg Pike, Colonel Thomas J. Henderson's brigade went into position—commanded today by Colonel Israel N. Stiles, due to Colonel Henderson's being ill. Cox considered this part of the line critical since a breakthrough on the Lewisburg Pike would put the Confederates nearer the vital bridges than most of the rest of the Federal army. Stiles's brigade would cover a front of about 250 yards.

Left: Brigadier General Jacob D. Cox, commander, Third Division, Federal XXIII Corps. A lawyer from Ohio, Cox was temporarily given command of the XXIII Corps at Franklin and made his headquarters at the Carter House. Cox directed the preparation of the defenses and commanded the Federal main line during the battle. *Library of Congress*.

Below: Carter cotton gin and press house as seen from Columbia Pike, circa 1880s. This was the scene of some of the most vicious fighting of the war when Major General Patrick Cleburne's division attacked the Federal line at the cotton gin across this ground. Brigadier General Hiram Granbury was killed on or near the pike, and Cleburne was killed about fifty yards in front of the cotton gin. *U.S. Army Military History Institute*.

Colonel John S. Casement's brigade took a position on Stiles's right and covered the ground between the Lewisburg Pike and the eastern edge of the Carter cotton gin property, a distance of almost four hundred yards. The remaining distance from the cotton gin to the pike, a little over one hundred yards, was covered by James Reilly's brigade. Because of the relatively short distance, Reilly put two regiments on the line with his remaining three regiments along the slope of the hill, about fifty yards in the rear. Later in the day, a four-gun Kentucky battery would go into position with Reilly's men covering the pike. With the large gin house on his left and the passage of the pike through the lines on his right, Reilly's position was sure to attract a lot of attention.

While each of Reilly's regiments set to work fortifying their positions, the remainder of the XXIII Corps—Thomas Ruger's division—began arriving, and General Cox put the men to work extending the line west of the Columbia Pike. Colonel Silas A. Strickland's brigade went into position with his two veteran regiments on the front line—the 50th Ohio extending west from the pike for about fifty yards and the 72nd Illinois then angling back through Mr. Carter's garden for another one hundred yards or so. From that point, Orlando Moore's brigade of seven regiments covered the last six hundred yards or so on to Carter's Creek Pike. Since Ruger's division was understrength, two new regiments had been added to Strickland's brigade, and they occupied a retrenchment line behind Strickland and Moore's front line for about three hundred yards—the 44th Missouri beginning in the Carter backyard and the 183rd Ohio extending the line on to the west.

Sixty-seven-year-old Fountain Branch Carter had seen a lot of things since he built his fine brick house on the Columbia Pike south of Franklin thirty-four years earlier, but nothing like this. The Federals had occupied Franklin and stationed a few thousand troops there, off and on, for the last two and a half years. They had even built an earthen fort named for general Gordon Granger on the bluffs just north of the river to cover the railroad bridge, and they fought a couple small engagements within a mile or so of his house. But this was different. Carter had been awakened before dawn, and Brigadier General Cox had set up a field headquarters in his parlor. Now, two divisions were camping on Carter's property and throwing up breastworks while thousands more soldiers, with their wagons and artillery, streamed past Carter's house on the way into town. Fountain Branch and his eldest son, Lieutenant Colonel Moscow Carter, a Confederate officer who was home on parole from a Federal prison

Fountain Branch Carter, owner of the Carter House. Mr. Carter led a group of at least twenty-five noncombatants, including fifteen members of his own family, who survived by hiding in his basement. One of Carter's sons, a Confederate officer, was mortally wounded in his garden. *Battle of Franklin Trust, Carter House collection.*

camp, decided to keep the family close to the house but had everybody pack a small bag in case they had to leave quickly.[49]

With Ruger's division in place, Cox had covered what he considered the most likely areas for a Confederate attack. Reilly's position east of the pike was a strong one, while Ruger's line west of the pike was considerably thinner but should still hold. Ruger's line, however, ended at Carter's Creek Pike, which left over a half mile of undefended ground between Ruger's right flank and the river. Cox did not think that the Confederates could move an infantry force far enough to threaten it before dark, but he was concerned that Forrest's cavalry could find the open flank and attack Ruger's rear. Cox pointed this out to Schofield, and soon Brigadier General Nathan Kimball's division of the IV Corps, which was just arriving, was sent to fill the gap in the line.

Also about this time, the artillery began to arrive. Schofield had ordered the XXIII Corps artillery to be taken across the river as soon as it arrived, promising Cox that he would be given IV Corps guns as they came in. By late morning, Captain Lyman Bridges, chief of artillery for the IV Corps, reported to Cox for orders and began to put the guns in position. By the time the battle opened, there would be about thirty Federal guns in place in the main line or just behind. In addition to the IV Corps guns, after crossing the river, Captain Giles J. Cockerill, XXIII Corps artillery chief, put his own battery into position in Fort Granger. Even from across the river, Cockerill's three-inch ordnance rifles had the range to support Stiles's brigade on the Federal left at the Lewisburg Pike. During the battle, they would fire 163 rounds.[50]

By midday on November 30, John Schofield's situation at Franklin was much improved. Brigadier General Cox's defensive line on the south edge of town was shaping up nicely—three divisions were in place, the breastworks were almost finished, the artillery was arriving and the wagon train was at least within the lines. The repairs on the old bridge had been completed, and it was in use for troops and soon would be for wagons also. A fourth division—Thomas J. Wood's from the IV Corps—had already crossed the river and was taking up positions to cover the bridges and the wagons as they reached the north bank. Only Wagner's division—the rear guard—remained outside the lines as it continued to skirmish with the lead units of the Confederate army south of town near Winstead Hill. In another encouraging development, after almost forty-eight hours, Schofield was back in contact with his cavalry.

Soon after arriving in Franklin, Schofield had received word that Major General Wilson and most of the mounted troops were a few miles east of town and were now covering the army's left flank and the Harpeth River crossings. Even with Wilson back in contact, however, Schofield's greatest concern remained Forrest's cavalry. This is clear from a message he sent to Nashville that morning:

> FRANKLIN, *November 30, 1864—9:50 a.m.*
> *Major-General THOMAS,*
> *Nashville:*
> *My trains are coming in all right. Half the troops are here, and the other half about five miles out, coming on in good order, with light skirmishing. I will have all across the river this evening. Wilson is here, and has his cavalry on my flank. I do not know where Forrest is; he may have gone east, but, no doubt, will strike our flank and rear again soon. Wilson is entirely unable to cope with him. Of course I cannot prevent Hood from crossing the Harpeth whenever he may attempt it. Do you desire me to hold on here until compelled to fall back?*
>
> *J.M. SCHOFIELD,*
> *Major-General.*[51]

By early afternoon, John Schofield was confident that he could get most of his supplies across the bridges by sundown and then withdraw the rest of the army so they could, as he had told Jacob Cox, "fight with the river in front of us." In response to a request from Thomas, Schofield had replied that, once across the Harpeth, he could probably hold Hood at Franklin for another day, but no more.[52] He had already issued orders for the men to begin falling back across the river as soon as it was dark.[53] The Confederates had forced his rear guard back off the hills south of town, and they had fallen back to within half a mile of the main line, but Schofield and most of his men believed that the rest of the afternoon would probably be taken up with little more than skirmishing. Major General David Stanley, commander of the IV Corps, wrote the following in his official report: "…in view of the strong position we held, and reasoning from the former course of the rebels during this campaign, nothing appeared so improbable as that they would assault. I felt so confident in this belief that I did not leave General Schofield's headquarters until the firing commenced."[54]

They were all wrong.[55]

THE CONFEDERATE APPROACH

Alexander P. Stewart's corps was on the road early that Wednesday morning, leading the Confederates north from Spring Hill in pursuit of the Federal army. At Thompson Station, they saw the evidence of "Sul" Ross's brigade's attack on the Federal column several hours earlier, with burned wagons and dead mules along the roadside. From that point on, signs of the fleeing troops littered the pike—broken wagons, dead animals and discarded military equipment and knapsacks, thrown away as the soldiers tried to lighten their loads. Up ahead, they could hear the sounds of gunfire and artillery as Forrest pressed the rear of the Federal column.

At about midday, Stewart's lead units caught up to Forrest's men about three miles south of Franklin. Up ahead, the pike ran through a gap in the ridgeline at Winstead Hill, and there, the Federal rear guard was posted with a section of artillery. Now that the infantry had arrived, Forrest took his cavalry to the right, toward the river, and a short time later, Hood ordered Stewart to move to the right also—to the Lewisburg Pike, about two miles away. This would outflank the Federal position at Winstead Hill and clear the way for Frank Cheatham's corps to advance on up Columbia Pike. By about 1:00 p.m., the Federal rear guard had withdrawn from the ridge and fallen back into the valley toward the Federal line near the Carter House.

Stewart's corps moved up the Lewisburg Pike and began spreading out to the west toward Columbia Pike. On Stewart's right, beginning at the pike, was Major General William W. Loring's division, with some of Forrest's dismounted cavalry (Buford's) between the pike and the river. In Stewart's center was the division of Major General Edward C. Walthall.

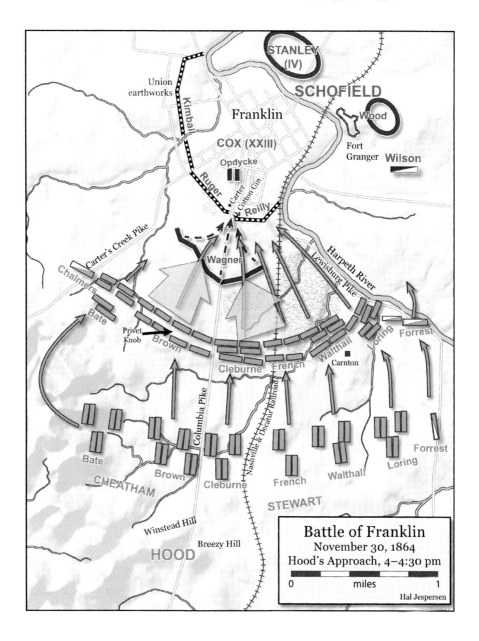

Battle of Franklin
November 30, 1864
Hood's Approach, 4–4:30 pm

0   miles   1

Hal Jespersen

Directly ahead of Walthall's and Loring's divisions was the fine home and plantation of John McGavock, called Carnton. Finally, on Stewart's left was the division of Major General Samuel G. French, understrength that day because one of his brigades (Ector's) was guarding the supply line south of Franklin. Because of the march to Spring Hill, Stewart only had one artillery battery (Guibor's Missouri battery) on the field. It was split into three two-gun sections to cover as much ground as possible.

While Stewart was moving up the Lewisburg Pike, Frank Cheatham's corps marched through the gap at Winstead Hill and began to deploy on Stewart's left. Major General Patrick R. Cleburne put his division between Samuel French's left and the Columbia Pike. Cleburne's division was also understrength, having left Brigadier General James A. Smith's brigade to convoy a supply train from the Tennessee River. On Cleburne's left, beginning at the Columbia Pike, was Major General John C. Brown's division. Finally, bringing up the rear of Cheatham's corps was the division of Major General William B. Bate, which would extend Brown's line on to the Carter's Creek Pike.

It was about 2:00 p.m. when Cheatham's corps began moving past Winstead Hill and deploying in the valley, but General Hood and some of the other senior Confederate commanders had been there somewhat earlier.[56] Soon after the Federal rear guard fell back, Hood and some of his staff rode up the slope of Winstead Hill and began to survey the Federal position, almost two miles away. About the same time, Cheatham and Cleburne did the same. All came away convinced that the Federal position was a strong one. After studying the enemy position for a time, Hood rode back down the hill and began sending couriers out to bring the senior commanders to a meeting. It was at that meeting that the fate of a great many men would be decided.

The first senior Confederate officer to get a close look at the Federal position at Franklin was Nathan Bedford Forrest. Shortly after noontime, Forrest, with some of his troops, had ridden over to the Lewisburg Pike and on to Carnton, John McGavock's home, where he observed the Federal lines from just under a mile away.[57] Forrest then rode back and found General Hood on Columbia Pike, about three miles from Franklin. Unfortunately, his report was not encouraging. In Forrest's opinion, the Federal position was too strong to assault without unacceptable losses. He proposed to take his cavalry and one infantry division across the river and turn the left flank of the Federal line. If Hood would agree, he promised to do it in two hours.

Even though Hood had not yet seen the Federal position for himself, he had already come to some conclusions. He told Forrest that he believed the Federals were continuing to retreat as fast as possible and that the show of force in their line that Forrest had seen was simply "a feint to hold me back from a more vigorous pursuit." Hood, it seems, had already decided that there would be no flanking movements today, telling Forrest instead that he didn't think the Federal position could stand "strong pressure from the front."[58] In fact, Hood was partially correct—Schofield's army was moving across the river as fast as possible. The strength of its defensive line, however, was not an illusion. All this had happened before Hood called his senior commanders together after returning from his own reconnaissance at Winstead Hill.

According to local tradition, Hood's meeting took place at the Harrison House, about half a mile south of Winstead Hill on Columbia Pike. It's not known exactly who was present, but the reactions of at least three senior officers to Hood's plan of attack are known. Forrest repeated his opinion that a frontal assault would be too costly and again offered to take an infantry division across the river and flank the Federals out of their position—which Hood again denied. Instead, Forrest was told to have his cavalry on both flanks of the army and be ready to follow up any success the main attack might have.

Both Frank Cheatham and Patrick Cleburne voiced serious reservations about an assault on the Federal line they had just seen from Winstead Hill. Cheatham had gotten a good look at the Federal position and simply said, "I don't like the looks of this fight." Cleburne said that an assault such as the one Hood was proposing would result in a "terrible and useless waste of life." Hood listened to everyone's comments, but his mind remained unchanged. "We will make the fight," he said.[59]

Ever since that day, historians have debated Hood's two critical decisions—to attack that afternoon even though a third of his army and the bulk of his artillery were not yet on the field, and to make a frontal assault on the Federal position instead of a flanking maneuver.[60] It is, of course, a matter of record that these decisions produced horrendous results for Hood's army at Franklin. It is not clear, however, that those results would have been as obvious to Hood—who, like Lee at Gettysburg, desperately wanted to believe that success was possible—as they are to us 150 years later.

Interestingly, most historians have sought to explain Hood's decisions as the natural result of his own physical problems and professional limitations rather than the dictates of the tactical situation on the field that afternoon. Some have suggested that Hood was an excellent brigade or even division commander but was simply out of his depth as the commander of an entire army. Others have suggested that, considering his wounds—a disabled left arm and an amputated right leg—perhaps his thinking was impaired by the use of liquor or other painkillers. Finally, there are those who believe that he was so blinded with anger over the failure at Spring Hill that he ordered the assault at Franklin out of spite—to teach his army a lesson, so to speak.

While Hood was young and certainly had his shortcomings as an army commander, the maneuver that he planned and executed at Spring Hill was not the work of a commander who lacked either imagination or tactical skill. The accusation that Hood might have been under the influence of either liquor or laudanum has no support in contemporary records and only appeared in print in the 1940s.[61] As to the last theory, while Hood was certainly angry about Spring Hill, there is likewise no evidence that he was so deluded or deranged that he ordered the assault at Franklin simply out of anger toward his officers and men. In fact, things that were completely out of his control probably had much more influence on Hood's decisions at Franklin than any personal or professional shortcomings.

At Franklin that afternoon, two things were obvious and likely dominated Hood's thinking. First, the Federal army was getting away. Hood correctly concluded that part of Schofield's army was already across the river and that the remainder would cross as soon as it was dark. Once across the Harpeth, they would be out of Hood's reach and within an easy day's march of Nashville, and any advantage Hood might have had would be lost. Franklin was Hood's last chance to meet Schofield on anything like even terms, but to take advantage of that, he must attack before dark.

Second, the sun was going down. Once it became obvious that he had to attack that afternoon or let Schofield escape (again), Hood came under tremendous time pressure. It was probably 2:30 p.m. or so when Hood's meeting broke up. At that point, there simply was not enough time to maneuver for anything other than a direct assault. It would take another half hour at least to get the orders to all the units. Cheatham's last division (Bate) had to march to its left and around a hill to get into position, which meant that Hood's entire line would not be ready before about 3:45 p.m.[62] As desperate a gamble as the frontal assault with only two of his infantry corps was, it's hard to see what other options Hood had in the time remaining before sundown, which would come at about 4:30 p.m. that day.

Major General John M. Schofield, commander of Federal forces at Spring Hill and Franklin. Commander of the Army of the Ohio during the Atlanta Campaign, Schofield was sent back to Tennessee and put in command of his own XXIII Corps, as well as David Stanley's IV Corps. These were the Federal troops who opposed Hood at Spring Hill and Franklin. *Library of Congress.*

Ironically, his opponent at Franklin seems to have seen Hood's situation more clearly than many of the historians who have come later. Thirty-three years after the battle, John Schofield would write in his biography the following:

> Hood's assault at Franklin has been severely criticized. Even so able a general as J.E. Johnston has characterized it as "a useless butchery." These criticisms are founded on a misapprehension of the facts and are essentially erroneous…It was impossible, after the pursuit from Spring Hill, in a short day to turn our position or make any other attack but a direct one in front.

After making some comments about the desperation of the Confederate cause by that point in the war, Schofield concludes:

> Franklin was the last opportunity he [Hood] could expect to have to reap the results hoped for in his aggressive movement. He must strike here, as best he could, or give up his cause as lost. I believe, therefore, that there can be no room for doubt that Hood's assault was entirely justifiable.[63]

In the end, whether the decision to make the frontal assault that afternoon was largely dictated by the tactical situation or by Hood's own personal issues, it made little difference. Everyone involved knew that it was still a desperate, long-odds gamble and that, win or lose, it would be brutal and bloody.

Shortly before 4:00 p.m., Hood's units were in place and moving forward. His line reached from the Harpeth River and the Lewisburg Pike on the east, across the Columbia Pike and on to the Carter's Creek Pike on the west. It was made up of six infantry divisions and was about two and a half miles long. Estimates of its strength range from sixteen thousand to eighteen thousand men. Forrest's three divisions of cavalry on the flanks (Buford and Jackson on the east and Chalmers on the west) added over four thousand more. The nearest Federal troops were about a mile away. There were seventeen regiments in the Federal main line between Carter's Creek Pike and the river, and all of them had skirmishers out as far as a half mile in front of their positions. In the center, however, there were more than skirmishers. Two of Brigadier General Wagner's brigades (Lane's and Conrad's) had, under Wagner's orders, formed an advanced line on either side of the Columbia Pike, about seven hundred yards in front of the main line near the Carter cotton gin.[64] Wagner's last brigade (Opdycke's), after a

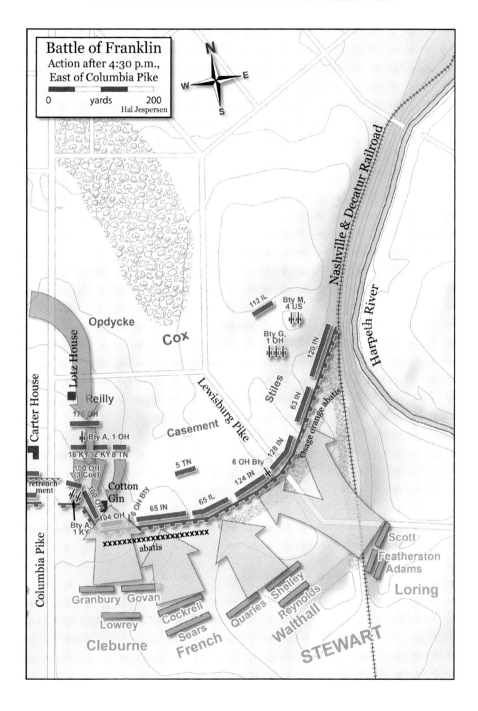

protest from its commander, was allowed to fall back inside the works and was resting about 150 yards behind the Carter House, acting as the reserves for the main line.

The waiting was over. Hood was coming with everything he had. Jacob Cox and his men had their backs to the Harpeth River. They had to hold their ground or be killed or captured. Hood believed—and had told his commanders—that "Franklin was the key to Nashville and Nashville is the key to independence." Franklin was a battle neither side could afford to lose, and for many of the men who were there and survived, it would haunt them for the rest of their lives.

Chapter 7

"Let Us Die Like Men"

THE EASTERN FLANK—STEWART'S CORPS

Alexander Peter Stewart was a native Tennessean and a West Point graduate (class of 1842). He had served for only three years after graduation when he resigned his commission and became a professor of mathematics at Cumberland University and, later, at the University of Nashville. Like a great many West Pointers who had gone back to civilian life, Stewart went back into service when the war broke out. He was commissioned a major of artillery in the Tennessee Militia and then in the Confederate army by August 1861. Stewart rose steadily in rank, becoming a major general and commanding a division by the summer of 1863. In June 1864, Stewart was promoted to lieutenant general and given command of Leonidas Polk's corps when the bishop was killed near Kennesaw Mountain during the Atlanta Campaign. Now, five months later, Stewart was commanding the Confederate right and sending his corps against Jacob Cox's line at Franklin on a beautiful Indian summer afternoon.

When Stewart's corps began to organize in the valley south of the Federal lines, there was plenty of room for his three divisions to deploy. As they began to move forward, however, the river began to narrow the field. On Stewart's right, William Loring's division advanced in a two-brigade front (Thomas Scott near the river and W.S. Featherston on his left) with John Adams's brigade in reserve. As they passed Carnton Plantation, the river began to force Scott to his left, into Featherston, and "funnel" Loring's division up the

Lewisburg Pike and into the guns of Israel Stiles's brigade, waiting behind their breastworks.

Loring's men had been under artillery fire for some time as they approached the Federal line, but as they came to within one hundred yards or so, a more formable obstacle appeared. Between them and the Federal line ran a hedge of Osage orange bushes. Major General Walthall, whose division was to Loring's left and encountered the same barrier in front of the Federal breastworks, said, "Over this, no organized force could go."[65] Here the momentum of Featherston and Scott's attack was broken, as individuals and small groups of men worked their way through the hedge, with officers hacking openings with their swords and men tearing their hands on the Osage orange thorns. It was here also that the Indiana troops of Stiles's brigade began to pour volley after volley of small arms fire into the Mississippi and Alabama men.

Lieutenant General Alexander P. Stewart, corps commander, Confederate Army of Tennessee. A steady, reliable officer, Stewart commanded three divisions during the Tennessee Campaign. *Alabama Department of Archives and History.*

Some of the Southern troops tried to flank the Federal line by following the Nashville & Decatur tracks down to the riverbank, but the guns in Fort Granger and Battery M of the Fourth U.S. Artillery turned the railroad cut into a slaughterhouse. Parts of three Mississippi regiments managed to cut their way through the thorn bushes and stormed the Federal works near the Lewisburg Pike but were beaten back. Brigadier General John Adams, commanding Loring's reserve brigade, saw the pileup in front of him and began to slide his brigade to its left, looking for a way through the hedge. Their time would come soon enough. Stiles's brigade held firm, and Loring's division would lose two of its three brigade commanders and eventually take about 25 percent casualties.

To Loring's left, Major General Edward Walthall's division crossed the same sort of ground and met the same Osage orange hedge, but his three brigades faced the Federal brigade commanded by Colonel John Casement. As the Confederate troops approached, Casement had yelled to his troops, "I want you to stand here like rocks and whip hell out of them," and now his Indiana and Illinois men did just that. Walthall's Alabama, Tennessee and Arkansas troops fought bravely but could not breach the Federal line. Walthall lost one of his brigade commanders and ten out of seventeen regimental commanders and had two horses shot under him. His division also suffered about 25 percent casualties. It was here in front of Walthall's position, however, that one of the most remarkable incidents of the battle happened.

Brigadier General John Adams was a career army officer, having graduated from West Point in 1846 along with classmates George McClellan, George Pickett and Thomas J. "Stonewall" Jackson. When the war began, Adams, like so many others, resigned his commission and joined the Confederacy. On this day, Adams commanded William Loring's reserve brigade, and as the two brigades in front of him piled up on the Osage orange hedge, he brought his men to the left, searching for a way to get to the Federal line. During this movement, Adams was wounded in the right shoulder but remained mounted. As they came into the area where Walthall's men were making their attack, Adams spotted a gap in the hedge and led his Mississippi troops toward it. As they formed up to attack, Adams rode to the front and suddenly spurred his horse, Old Charley, forward. Alone, out in front of his brigade, Adams rode straight for the Federal works.

On a field where brave men were already dying by the hundreds, all who saw Adams—Federal and Confederate alike—were stunned. Amazingly, it looked as though Adams was going to try to leap the breastworks! Adams and Old Charley made it all the way to the Federal line before being shot down in front of the Sixty-fifth Illinois' color guard. Old Charley fell across the parapet with Adams pinned under him, but as soon as there was a lull in the fighting, the Illinois men carried Adams back behind their lines, where he died of his wounds. Colonel John Casement had Adams's watch and ring returned to his widow and took Old Charley's saddle home with him when the war ended. Adams's brigade followed its commander to the Federal works but, like the other Confederate units, was unable to take them.[66]

On Stewart's left, his last—and smallest—division kept pace with the others as they closed on the Federal line. Commanded by Major General Samuel G. French, a West Point classmate of Ulysses S. Grant, this division had left one brigade guarding the supply train and only numbered about 1,500 men that afternoon. As Stewart's corps attacked, French's division was the only one to have any contact with the Federal advanced line, with part of Brigadier General Claudius Sears's brigade hitting Joseph Conrad's left flank. French's other unit, the Missouri brigade under Brigadier General Francis M. Cockrell, surged on past Conrad's men and saw that they were past most of the Osage orange hedge and had an almost unimpeded path toward the Federal line. In fact, since the rest of Stewart's units were temporarily held up by the thorny obstacle, Cockrell's Missourians may well have been the first Confederate unit to actually reach the Federal breastworks. If so, they paid dearly for the honor.

Cockrell's Missouri brigade, almost seven hundred strong, faced John Casement's right flank, the Sixty-fifth Indiana, which was supported by two twelve-pound Napoleons from the Sixth Ohio artillery. The guns fired through openings cut in the breastworks and were commanded by Lieutenant Aaron P. Baldwin. As they approached the Federal line, Cockrell's men walked into an inferno of fire and lead. At least one company of the Sixty-fifth Indiana was armed with fifteen-shot Henry repeaters, and Baldwin's guns fired as fast as his men could load—double and triple canister and then improvised loads made up of soldier's socks filled with rifle bullets. Scores of Cockrell's officers and men were cut down in the open ground in front of Baldwin's guns, and then it became a hand-to-hand fight as the survivors tried to force their way over the works and through the artillery embrasures. Baldwin's gunners fought with axes and picks and fired point blank into the Confederates crowding the gun ports. Baldwin later told another officer that he could hear two distinct sounds when his guns fired—the explosion and then the cracking of the bones.[67]

By now, all three divisions of Stewart's corps were engaged from the river almost to the cotton gin. Stewart's entire line would become a killing field, but none of his units would suffer like the Missouri brigade. Within a few minutes, John Casement's men and Aaron Baldwin's guns practically destroyed Cockrell's brigade as a functioning unit. Over 75 percent of the brigade's officers were killed, wounded or captured, including Cockrell and all of his regimental commanders. Overall, the Missourians suffered 60 percent casualties, the highest of any brigade on either side.

On the eastern flank, along a front of about six hundred yards, A.P. Stewart's three divisions were being mauled by two Federal brigades and their artillery support. In the center and west of the Columbia Pike, however, the drama was just beginning.

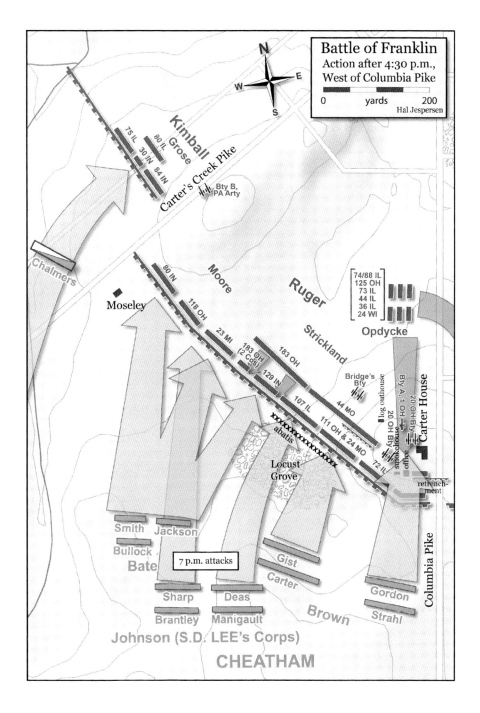

WESTERN FLANK—CHEATHAM'S CORPS

Thirty-six-year-old Patrick Ronayne Cleburne was born in County Cork, Ireland, and, as a young man, had served three years in the British army. By 1850, he had immigrated to the United States and settled in Helena, Arkansas, where he became a pharmacist and a lawyer. By 1855, he was a naturalized citizen. When Arkansas seceded, Cleburne was elected colonel of the Fifteenth Arkansas regiment but was soon promoted to brigadier general, commanding a brigade at Shiloh. By the end of 1862, he was a major general, commanding a division at Stones River.

Patrick Cleburne had served in the Army of Tennessee since it was formed and had become, by common consent, its finest division commander. On this day, however, Cleburne was worried. He had opposed the frontal assault he was about to lead, seeing only "a terrible and useless loss of life." Once given his orders, however, he promised General Hood that he would "take the works or fall in the effort." According to Daniel Govan, one of his brigade commanders, Cleburne returned to his division "more despondent than I ever saw him." On hearing the orders, Govan said that not many of them would make it back to Arkansas. "Well, Govan," Cleburne answered, "if we are to die, let us die like men."[68] Now, as it approached 4:00 p.m., Cleburne's division was going forward to attack.

Cleburne's men formed the right flank of Frank Cheatham's corps and advanced with Samuel French's division on their right and the Columbia Pike on their left. For a while, they kept in line with French's men and the rest of Stewart's corps to their right, but they soon closed on the Federal advanced line almost half a mile in front of the main works. The presence of the Federal advanced line was no surprise to the Confederates—they had all seen it from Winstead Hill. In fact, Cleburne and John Brown, commanding the division to Cleburne's left, were counting on it being there since it was part of their plan. On the Federal side of the advanced line, however, things were becoming tense.

Colonel Joseph Conrad's brigade held the eastern half of the advanced line (facing Cleburne) with about 1,500 men, while Colonel John Q. Lane held the western half (facing Brown) with about 1,500 more. Conrad had only been in command of his brigade for about twenty-four hours, while Lane had been in command less than thirty-six hours. They had understood, from Brigadier General Wagner, their division commander, that they would be withdrawn from their exposed position if an attack developed. But they had received no orders, and now Hood's entire army was coming. A courier

Brigadier General George D. Wagner, commander, Second Division, Federal IV Corps. It was Wagner's division that defended Spring Hill and made up the rear guard on the march to Franklin. Wagner's second and third brigades were left out in an advanced line at Franklin, leading to a breach in the Federal main line when they were overrun and fell back. Wagner's first brigade, however, came forward and helped to stop the breakthrough. *Library of Congress.*

was rushed back to the main line with a request to fall back. Wagner, exhausted from thirty-six hours of marching and fighting and badly bruised from a horse fall, could not yet see the advancing Confederates from his position at the main line, and so he sent the courier back with orders for Conrad and Lane to stand and fight. Now completely confused, Conrad and Lane prepared to do their best against what appeared to be overwhelming odds.[69]

As Stewart's men swept on toward the Federal main line on their right, Cleburne's skirmish line began to engage Conrad's men east of the pike while Brigadier General George W. Gordon's brigade from Brown's division engaged Lane's men on the west side. The Federal's first volley staggered the Confederates and sent them back under cover for a short time, but then they came back much stronger, and within a few minutes, the Federal advance line was in serious trouble. Suddenly, one regiment broke and others followed, and the Federal line came apart, starting a stampede as the Federal troops ran for their lives.[70] This was what the Confederates had hoped for.

As they came forward that afternoon, Cleburne and Brown's divisions planned to use the advanced line that the Federals had foolishly left in place to their advantage. They planned to break that line and then press the survivors back into their main line, using them as a sort of shield from the enemy fire. Captain Samuel Foster of the Twenty-fourth Texas Cavalry (dismounted) remembered it like this:

> *…as soon as they break to run, our men break after them. They have nearly one-half mile to run to get back to their next line—so here we go right after them and yelling like fury and shooting at them at the same time. Kill some*

of them before they reach their works, and those that are in the second line of works are not able to shoot us because their own men are in front of us…So here we go, Yanks running for life and we for the fun of it.[71]

The men in the main line, who had seen the advanced line break, now saw a mob of six to seven thousand men come running back toward them, and they did hold their fire as long as they could, letting as many of their men get in as possible. For the Confederates, however, the "fun," as Captain Foster put it, ended about one hundred yards out when four Federal regiments stood up and opened fire. Over thirty years later, General Gordon, commanding one of John Brown's brigades, recalled:

When they fled, the shout was raised by some of the charging Confederates: "Go into the works with them! Go into the works with them!" This cry was quickly caught up and wildly vociferated from a thousand straining throats as we rushed on after the flying forces we had routed, killing some in our running fire, capturing others who were slow of foot, and sustaining but little loss ourselves until, perhaps, within a hundred paces of their main line and stronghold, when it seemed to me that hell itself had exploded in our faces…It yet seems a mystery and a wonder how any of us ever reached the works alive.[72]

In fact, many of the Confederates did reach the works, and unlike Stewart's men farther east, some were able to get through. Brown's men overwhelmed the Fiftieth Ohio on the west side of the pike and pushed them through Mr. Carter's garden and into his back yard. When the Fiftieth Ohio broke, the Seventy-second Illinois, just to the west, was outflanked and had to fall back as well. For about 150 yards west of the pike, the Federal main line held by Silas Strickland's two veteran regiments collapsed. In front of the cotton gin, however, Cleburne's men were taking a beating from James Reilly's Ohio, Kentucky and Tennessee troops. Fire raked them from the works ahead, as well as from Baldwin's guns and some of the Sixty-fifth Indiana's rifles to their right. An Illinois soldier near the gin house later wrote: "I was a reenlisted veteran and went through twenty-seven general engagements, but I am sure that Franklin was the hardest fought field I ever stood upon…I never saw men in such a terrible position as Cleburne's Division was in for a few minutes. The wonder is that any of them escaped death or capture."[73]

Some of Cleburne's men went over the works held by the 104th Ohio, while others went through on the pike and captured a Kentucky artillery

Franklin battlefield looking south along Columbia Pike, circa 1880s. This picture was taken just over one hundred yards south of the Carter House—just in front of the position held by the Fiftieth Ohio. The cotton gin is just out of view to the left, across the pike. Wagner's advanced line was along the small ridge in the distance. *U.S. Army Military History Institute.*

battery supported by the 100th Ohio. For a few minutes, Cleburne's troops and the men of the two Ohio regiments were involved in a fight that was more like a back-alley brawl than a military operation, as hundreds of men in blue and gray jammed into the small area around the cotton gin—using any weapon that came to hand and killing anyone wearing the wrong color shirt. The tide soon turned against the Southerners, however, as Reilly's three reserve regiments ran down the slope behind the cotton gin and joined the fight. In the end, all of Cleburne's men who broke the Federal line were killed, captured or forced back over the works.[74]

Pat Cleburne had made good on his promise, but the cost was terrible. His men had taken the works, at least temporarily, but as he predicted, many died in the effort, including Cleburne himself. He was last seen on foot, after his second horse had been killed, leading men forward into the smoke. His body was found the next morning about fifty yards from the cotton gin.[75] Leading Cleburne's Texas brigade, Brigadier General Hiram Granbury died near the pike, and twelve regimental commanders were killed, wounded or captured. Cleburne's division as a whole suffered an appalling 51 percent casualties.[76]

Left: Colonel Emerson Opdycke, commander, first brigade, Wagner's division, Federal IV Corps. When the Confederates broke through the Federal main line at the Columbia Pike, Colonel Opdycke brought his reserve brigade forward into the area around the Carter House, playing a crucial role in stopping the breakthrough and restoring the Federal line. *Library of Congress.*

Right: Major General Patrick R. Cleburne, division commander, Confederate Army of Tennessee. A British army veteran and Irish immigrant, Cleburne was probably the finest division commander in the Western Theater, and his men were the primary Confederate infantry engaged at Spring Hill. At Franklin the next day, Cleburne was killed leading his men against the cotton gin. *Library of Congress.*

While Cleburne's men fought hand to hand around the cotton gin, John Brown's men surged up through Fountain Branch Carter's garden toward his house, where the survivors of the Seventy-second Illinois, the Fiftieth Ohio and the Forty-fourth Missouri were trying to form a new defensive line. Hiding in the basement of the house were at least twenty-five civilians, including Mr. Carter and fifteen members of his family. As the Confederates surged into the Carter yard, the beleaguered men from the front line received some desperately need help. Running into the yard and along Columbia Pike from the other direction, Emerson Opdycke's reserve brigade arrived. The men had been resting in a field near the home of Johann Albert Lotz when they saw some of Wagner's men from the advance line running past them into town and heard the rising sound of the battle. Knowing something had gone wrong, they went forward before orders could be issued

Major General David S. Stanley, commander, Federal IV Corps at Spring Hill and Franklin. Stanley held the town of Spring Hill with one division and then brought up the rear while the rest of the Federal army escaped to Franklin. Wounded the next day at Franklin, Stanley was later awarded the Medal of Honor for his actions. *Library of Congress.*

The backyard of the Carter House today. The original buildings are (from left to right) the main house, the kitchen, the farm office (red wooden building) and the brick smokehouse. At the height of the battle, almost four thousand men fought in this yard. *Author's collection.*

and arrived just in time to meet the Confederate breakthrough. Along with them came IV Corps commander Major General David Stanley, riding in from the town, and temporary XXIII Corps commander Brigadier General Jacob Cox, who had just arrived from the eastern end of the line. Within a few minutes, Stanley was wounded and his horse killed. Jacob Cox then mounted Stanley on one of his own horses and sent him to the rear. It was now approaching 4:30 p.m., and troops were engaged for almost 1,500 yards along the Federal line.[77]

It was now a few minutes before sundown, and there were at least four thousand men in Mr. Carter's yard. The fighting there was hand to hand and desperate almost beyond belief, and the noise was deafening. One of the children in the basement later said that it was so loud that she couldn't hear herself scream. Even though these were modern nineteenth-century armies, a Roman legionnaire or a Greek hoplite would have felt at home in Mr. Carter's yard or around his cotton gin, fighting hand to hand, one man's strength against another's. Men killed and maimed one another with every conceivable weapon, and no one who was there ever forgot it. The regimental history of the Seventy-third Illinois put it this way:

> *The contending elements of Hell turned loose would seem almost as a Methodist love feast compared to the pandemonium that reigned there for the*

space of ten or twenty minutes. The scenes that we witnessed during that short space of time were so indelibly stamped upon the minds of the participants that even a long life…will not suffice to erase or even dim them.[78]

Among the men fighting in the Carter yard was an officer who was destined to become the father of a famous son. Nineteen-year-old Major Arthur MacArthur Jr. led the Twenty-fourth Wisconsin into Mr. Carter's backyard and was wounded three times but survived. Thirty-nine years later, his twenty-three-year-old son, Douglas MacArthur, graduated first in his class at West Point.

While the fight was going on in the Carter yard, a few hundred yards to the west, most of two Confederate divisions attacked the line held by Colonel Orlando Moore with one reinforced Federal brigade. Part of John C. Brown's division worked its way through a grove of locust trees and assaulted the east end of Colonel Moore's line, while William Bate's division hit the west end, closer to Carter's Creek Pike. While all the Confederate divisions suffered serious losses, none suffered the damage to its senior command structure as did John C. Brown's. That afternoon, the top two levels of the division command structure were wiped away. Brown himself was wounded, and

The Carter House today. *Photo by Allen Corry.*

of his four brigade commanders, Brigadier Generals Otho F. Strahl and States Rights Gist were killed; Brigadier General John C. Carter was mortally wounded, dying ten days later; and Brigadier General George W. Gordon was captured. Over all, Brown's division suffered about 31 percent casualties.

Major General William B. Bate's division was on the western end of Hood's line near Carter's Creek Pike and suffered the lightest casualties. There was, however, a young officer in one of Bate's brigades who had a special interest in the battle. Captain Theodrick "Tod" Carter, aide to Brigadier General Thomas Benton Smith, was the twenty-four-year-old son of Fountain Branch Carter, whose fine brick house now sat on a small hill a few hundred yards away as the brigade formed up for the attack. Telling General Smith that he had not been home in three years

Captain Theodrick "Tod" Carter, aide to Brigadier General Thomas Benton Smith, CSA. Born at the Carter House in 1840, Captain Carter was mortally wounded while attacking Federal troops entrenched in his father's garden. He died two days later in the house where he was born. *Battle of Franklin Trust, Carter House collection.*

but was "going home today," Captain Carter requested permission to return to his regiment—the Twentieth Tennessee—and join the assault. The permission was granted, and Captain Carter led men toward the Federal line where it ran through his father's garden. Carter's horse was killed, and he was wounded nine times, including one head wound above his left eye. Young Carter lay unconscious within two hundred yards of his own back porch all night. Before dawn the next morning, with the help of General Smith and some soldiers, Mr. Carter found his son on the battlefield and brought him to the house, where he was attended by a Confederate surgeon. A day later, however, Captain Tod Carter died of his wounds in his own home—across the hall from the room where he was born.[79] Over all, Bate's division suffered about 15 percent casualties.

Earlier in the day, Hood had denied Forrest's request to lead a flanking maneuver and instead ordered his cavalry to protect the army's flanks. Even so, that didn't keep him completely out of the fight. As the infantry was going forward, Forrest crossed to the east side of the Harpeth River with two of his divisions (Buford's and Jackson's). On this day, however—for the first time in the campaign—James Wilson and the Federal cavalry were ready for him, eventually driving Forrest and his men back across the river. To the west, James Chalmers's men skirmished with Nathan Kimball's line west of Carter's Creek Pike, but overall, Forrest's cavalry had little impact on the outcome of the battle. Forrest reported only 269 casualties for the entire month of November, so his losses at Franklin were slight—probably 100 men or fewer.[80]

It was now nearing 5:00 p.m., and the light was dying out over the field, which was already obscured by smoke. The breakthrough along the Columbia Pike at the Carter House had been stopped and turned back, thanks to the determination of the men from the front line who had fallen back but then stood their ground in the Carter yard, reinforced at the critical moment by Emerson Opdycke's fresh troops, who helped turn the tide. As darkness settled over the field, the Federal line was holding everywhere. From the Confederate command posts, south of the line, all that could be seen was a solid line of fire that stretched for almost a mile. General Hood, however, was not finished.

At about 5:00 p.m., S.D. Lee's leading division under Major General Ed Johnson finally reached the field and was immediately sent forward to Frank Cheatham's command post. Cheatham had no staff officers left to guide Johnson's division into position but pointed to the line of fire, half a mile in front of him, and said that Johnson's men were needed there as soon as possible because "the slaughter has been terrible with my brave men." By now, the sun was down, and moving Johnson's division through the fields and into position in the darkness took over an hour. It was about 7:00 p.m. when Johnson's men moved over ground that Bate's men had covered earlier and attacked Colonel Moore's line again, but they only added to the carnage without any more success than those before them had achieved. In fact, Johnson's division suffered more than Bate's division that had attacked in the daylight, taking about 21 percent casualties.[81]

Once darkness fell on the field at Franklin, the battle continued across the breastworks. The Federal troops held the inside of the works while thousands and thousands of Confederates—living and dead—were piled up along the outside. The two armies were now separated by only a few feet and fought

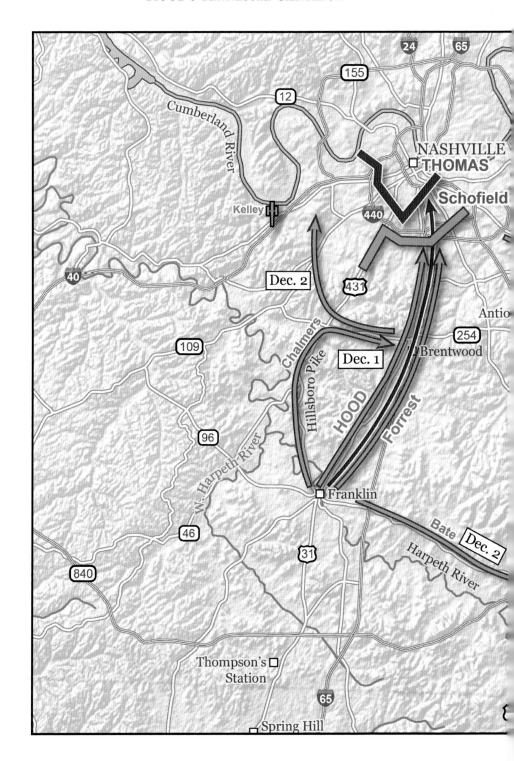

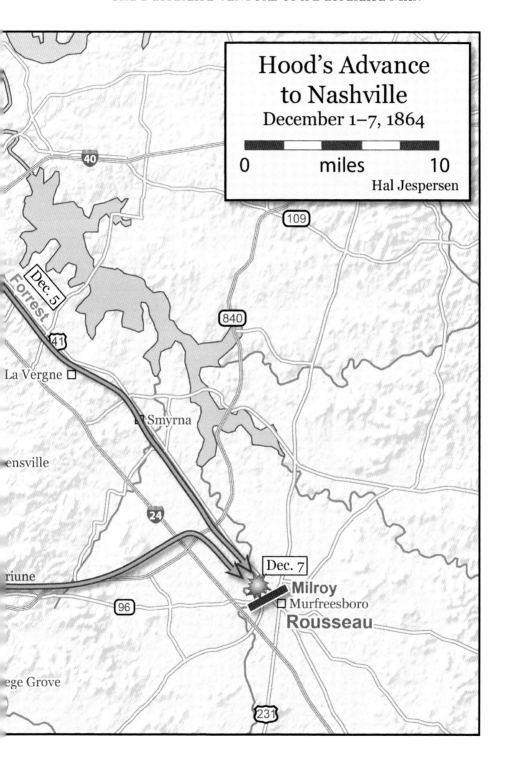

hand to hand over the works in the darkness. One Confederate described the situation on his side of the line this way:

> *Two lines of men fought with but a pile of dirt between them. In firing, the muzzles of the guns would pass each other, and nine times out of ten, when a man rose to fire, he fell back dead. It is to be remembered that the troops were all in confusion, that there were no organized commands. Officers and soldiers had straggled forward to this point of certain and swift death and they determined to kill as many as possible in the few minutes they had to live.*[82]

The battle continued like this along one part of the line or another for the next four hours. For those who survived, it would become the raw material of nightmares as long as they lived. One Federal soldier would later write the following in a letter home: "Franklin Tennessee: These are words that will haunt me the rest of my life."[83]

Chapter 8

Hood's Advance to Nashville

… grasping at the last straw.

The fighting at Franklin had ended around 9:00 p.m., and by midnight, the Federal troops received orders to fall back quietly, cross the river and march on to Nashville, as they had planned to do before the battle started. Still in command at the front line, Jacob Cox protested the order. Knowing how much Hood's army had suffered, Cox argued that they should hold their position and finish off the Confederates the following morning, before they could recover from the shock and disorganization of the past few hours. Cox was overruled, however, and the withdrawal began. All the statistics of the battle weigh heavily in favor of the Federal forces, but by withdrawing during the night, they left the field in the possession of the Confederates. This allowed Hood to claim Franklin as a victory—albeit a very expensive one.[84]

By sunup on December 1, the last of Schofield's army was across the river and moving on to Nashville. What under normal circumstances would have been an easy eighteen-mile march now became an endurance test. The Sixty-third Indiana, Stiles's brigade, was one of the last XXIII Corps units to leave and formed part of the corps rear guard. First Lieutenant James Pressnall, Company F, later wrote:

> *In the night march from Franklin to Nashville, our regiment, by reason of its worn down condition and loss of sleep, were entirely unfitted to properly*

perform the duties assigned it as rear guard of our retreating army. We had all we could do to take care of ourselves. With utmost care taken to keep our men on their feet and in line of march, we lost three during the night, who were picked up by the advancing enemy.[85]

Once across the Harpeth River, Schofield's infantry was able to march on to Nashville without being molested, which was fortunate since many of the troops were at the point of exhaustion. One Federal officer who fought in the front line later wrote: "While walking and engaged in conversation, sometimes in the middle of a sentence I would drop off to sleep and would stumble and almost fall, which would wake me and I would try to pick up the thread of the conversation…feeling very foolish."[86]

When they finally arrived at the fortifications at Nashville, many of the men in Schofield's army had been awake and on their feet for almost sixty hours. During that time, they had marched forty miles, fought two engagements and dug almost a mile of entrenchments. Even though they had been pushed to the point of collapse, they had also accomplished their mission of delaying Hood's advance long enough for reinforcements to arrive in Nashville.

George Henry Thomas was something of a rarity among the senior Federal commanders—a Virginian who did not go with his native state. Thomas graduated from West Point in 1840 with his friend and current commander William T. Sherman and three years ahead of Ulysses S. Grant. Unlike both Grant and Sherman, however, Thomas remained in the army until the outbreak of the war. Partly because of some early skepticism as to his loyalty, Thomas was slower

Major General George H. Thomas, commander of Federal forces in Tennessee. A Virginian who stayed loyal to the Union, Thomas was one of the North's best and most reliable commanders. He directed the Federal response to Hood's campaign and personally commanded the Federal troops who destroyed Hood's army at Nashville. *Library of Congress.*

to be promoted and was now junior to both men. After the fall of Atlanta, Thomas had been sent back to Nashville to defend Tennessee while Sherman planned his famous "March to the Sea." When Thomas arrived in Nashville on about the first of October, there was a considerable number of troops spread throughout the state, but the city itself was held by only about eight thousand garrison troops—primarily from the quartermaster department.

When Hood had marched away from the Tennessee River on November 21, Schofield's army constituted George Thomas's largest force in the field, with the city of Nashville itself still being held by only a small garrison, but that was only temporary. Thomas had been promised Major General A.J. Smith's XVI Corps from Missouri—over ten thousand men—but they were not able to leave St. Louis until November 22.[87] Over the next week, as the campaign progressed up through Columbia and Spring Hill, Thomas anxiously hoped

Major General Andrew J. Smith, commander, Federal XVI Corps. Smith brought his troops from Missouri to reinforce Thomas at Nashville. He moved his entire corps on riverboats from St. Louis, and his men began arriving at Nashville as the Battle of Franklin was underway. Two weeks later, they would play a large part in the destruction of Hood's army. *Library of Congress.*

for Smith's men to arrive every day. Finally, as the battle was going on at Franklin on November 30, the first of the XVI Corps troops began unloading at the docks on the Cumberland River at Nashville, with the rest arriving the following day.

The damage that Schofield inflicted on Hood's army at Franklin and the arrival of the XVI Corps at Nashville proved to be the turning point in the campaign. Even considering Schofield's losses at Franklin, during the twenty-four hours beginning on the afternoon of November 30, the balance of power in and around Nashville swung by at least fourteen thousand men in George Thomas's favor, with more Federal troops to come. After John Schofield's exhausted troops staggered in from the battlefield at Franklin, and the last of A.J. Smith's men disembarked at the landing, Thomas had almost thirty-five thousand men at Nashville, not counting James Wilson's cavalry. After the beating he had taken at Franklin, Hood would be lucky to field twenty-one thousand effective infantry.

It seemed that John Bell Hood was committed to fight to the finish at Franklin. During the night, he had moved his artillery into position and was prepared to open a bombardment at dawn, followed by an attack with his remaining forces, but, mercifully, the Federal line was empty. Now, as the Federal army marched away on that Thursday morning, the senior Confederate commanders began to get a look at the battlefield at Franklin for the first time. Major General Frank Cheatham, whose troops hit the center of the Federal line and were then caught up in the caldron around the cotton gin and in the Carter yard, was probably the first senior commander to ride to the front lines, just before dawn. Cheatham was a tough-as-nails veteran who had seen war in Mexico and on most of the major battlefields of the Western Theater. He had earlier told an aide, "This is a mistake, and it is no comfort to me to say that we [Hood's subordinate commanders] are not responsible." After three and a half years of war, Cheatham was no stranger to carnage, but nothing had prepared him for this. A soldier from the Nineteenth Tennessee reported seeing Cheatham walking along the pike near the federal line, holding a torch. The soldier said that "great big tears ran down his cheeks, as he looked into the faces of dead friends and listened to the cries of hundreds of his wounded men."[88]

Over twenty years later, Cheatham remembered his first look at the battlefield at Franklin:

> *Just at daybreak, I rode upon the field, and such a sight I never saw and can never expect to see again. The dead were piled up like stacks of wheat or scattered about like sheaves of grain. You could have walked all over the field upon dead bodies without stepping upon the ground...Almost under your eye, nearly all the dead, wounded and dying lay. In front of the Carter house, the bodies lay in heaps, and to the right of it, a locust thicket had been mowed off by bullets, as if by a scythe. It was a wonder that any man escaped alive...I never saw anything like that field, and never want to again.[89]*

The casualty numbers at Franklin are still in some dispute, even after 150 years. The Federal casualties, as officially reported, seem pretty straightforward: 2,326. According to recent research, however, the actual number might have been closer to 2,500. The long-accepted numbers for Hood's casualties come not from Confederate sources but from estimates made by the Federal army when it retook Franklin on December 18. There they found 3,800 wounded men and an estimated 1,750 field burials. To this they added the 702 Confederates captured during the battle and arrived at a figure of 6,252. Other evidence, however, indicates that the real number is probably closer to 7,000.[90]

As serious as the total Confederate losses were, what is striking is the ratio of Confederate dead to total casualties and the losses among the senior leadership. For most Civil War battles, Confederate dead would account for 15–18 percent of their total casualties, occasionally rising to 20 percent in a battle like Gettysburg. At Franklin, at least 28 percent of the Confederate casualties were dead on the field. In absolute numbers, more Confederates died at Franklin in five hours than died at Shiloh in two days. Hood, with something over 20,000 infantry engaged, lost 500 more men killed than Ambrose Burnsides did in the frontal assaults at Fredericksburg with 114,000 men engaged!

Finally, Franklin devastated Hood's senior officer's corps. The next morning, four general officers (Adams, Cleburne, Granbury and Strahl) were found dead on the field and taken to Carnton—John McGavock's house, which had been turned to a field hospital—and laid out on the back porch. Brigadier General States Rights Gist died at another field hospital. Brigadier

Rear view of Carnton Plantation, circa 1900. Carnton, owned by John McGavock, was the largest of the Confederate field hospitals after the Battle of Franklin. At one time, four dead Confederate generals were laid out on the large back porch. *Battle of Franklin Trust, Carnton collection.*

General John Carter was mortally wounded and died ten days later. Seven more generals were wounded and taken from the field, and one (George W. Gordon) was captured. In addition, fifty-five regimental commanders were killed, wounded or captured, making at least sixty-nine senior officers as casualties the next morning.

General Hood rode up the Columbia Pike shortly after Cheatham and saw the same ghastly scene. One soldier saw Hood as he surveyed the area near the pike and the cotton gin and said that "for a considerable time he sat on his horse and wept like a child." He then rode on into town and dismounted in the yard of Mrs. William Sykes, where he sat in a chair and tried to decide what the army would do. Little Alice McPhail remembered seeing him there: "I remember going with Aunt Sallie over to Mrs. Sykes'…and we saw a man sitting in a chair in the yard. He looked so sad, and Grandpa told me it was Gen. Hood." Hardin Figuers, a young teenager, remembered seeing him too: "I distinctly remember seeing Gen. Hood riding down through the streets of Franklin with his wooden leg and his long, tawny mustache and whiskers. I…was much disappointed."[91]

However disappointed and saddened Hood might have been about the results at Franklin, critical decisions had to be made, and he lost little time in making them. After his losses at Franklin, Hood could have chosen to stay in place and go on the defensive behind the Harpeth River. He could also have decided to fall back to Columbia or even all the way to the Tennessee River, essentially ending the campaign. Instead, Hood chose to follow Schofield to Nashville and invest the city as best he could. For the rest of his life, Hood remained convinced that it was the best option open to him. In his memoirs, published after his death in 1879, he explained his thinking:

> *I could not afford to turn southward unless for the special purpose of forming a junction with the expected reinforcements from Texas, and with the avowed intention to march again upon Nashville. In truth, our army was in that condition which rendered it more judicious the men should face a decisive issue rather than retreat…I therefore determined to move upon Nashville, to entrench, to accept the chance of reinforcement from Texas and…to adopt the only feasible means of defeating the enemy with my reduced numbers, vis., to await his attack and, if favored by success, follow him into his works…The troops would, I believed, return better satisfied even after defeat if, in grasping for the last straw, they felt that a brave and vigorous effort had been made to save the country from disaster. Such, at the time, was my opinion, which I have since had no reason to alter.*[92]

Hood's decision to move on to Nashville and await either reinforcements or a Federal attack has been debated for the last 150 years.[93]

Forrest and his cavalry were the first Confederates to pursue Schofield's army, getting on the road by dawn. Since it was already on the western flank of the battlefield, James Chalmers's division was sent up the Hillsboro Pike, while Forrest, with Buford and Jackson's divisions, moved up Wilson Pike that parallels the Franklin Pike on the east. Chalmers met almost no resistance, but at Owens Crossroads (present-day Concord Road at Wilson Pike), Forrest met most of a Federal cavalry brigade commanded by Brigadier General John H. Hammond.[94] After a brief engagement, however, Forrest's artillery and a charge by Buford's men sent the Federals back toward Nashville. Later that day, Forrest and Chalmers met near Brentwood but were too late to catch any of Schofield's army except a few stragglers.

By just after midday on December 1, Confederate infantry was also on the way up the Franklin Pike. S.D. Lee's corps, which was still relatively intact, crossed the river and marched on toward Nashville. By the end of the day, Stewart's corps had moved across the Harpeth River and camped for the night, while Cheatham's corps, which had suffered the most, remained in Franklin, reorganizing and burying the dead. On December 2, Forrest sent Chalmers west to cover the Hillsboro, Hardin (Harding) and Charlotte Pikes as the infantry began to arrive and take up positions east and west of Franklin Pike. On December 3, Lieutenant Colonel David Kelley was sent with a detachment and some artillery to block traffic on the Cumberland River below the city. Once the infantry arrived, Forrest, with the balance of the cavalry, was sent east to operate against the Nashville & Chattanooga Railroad.

On the morning of December 2, as they were moving toward Nashville, Major General William Bate received orders to detach from the main force and lead his division east to Murfreesboro and destroy the railroad between there and Nashville. Bate was led to believe that Murfreesboro was not heavily defended, but he soon reported to Hood that the Federals had a substantial garrison there.[95] On December 4, Forrest was ordered to assist Bate and take overall command, and he began the move the next morning. Detaching Bate and Forrest to Murfreesboro left Hood with just over nineteen thousand effective infantry plus one thousand or so of Chalmers's cavalry to invest the city of Nashville, which George Thomas now held with over forty thousand infantry, not counting James Wilson's cavalry.[96]

As Forrest moved to Murfreesboro, he continued to disable the rail line, capturing a blockhouse and its defenders at La Vergne. Forrest and

Bate met that evening near Smyrna, where they were reinforced by two more brigades (Sears and Palmer). On December 6, they moved down to Murfreesboro. On the morning of December 7, two Federal brigades—about 3,100 men—under Major General Robert H. Milroy came out for a reconnaissance in force and met Forrest's troops near Overall Creek. Some of Forrest's infantry broke and ran, but Milroy did not press his advantage and fell back into the Federal fortifications. After that, Bate and his division were ordered back to Nashville, and Forrest remained at Murfreesboro with about five thousand men. He was still there eight days later, when he learned about the battle at Nashville.[97]

While Forrest and Bate were at Murfreesboro, the rest of Hood's army was going into position around the south edge of Nashville. Lee's corps,

Depot at Nashville with the state capitol on the hill in the background, circa 1864. *Library of Congress.*

the first to arrive, held the center, east and west of the Franklin Pike near where it crosses the present-day highway I-440. A.P. Stewart's corps arrived next and went in on Lee's left, stretching generally from the Granny White Pike to the Hillsboro Pike, with their left refused some distance to the south. Along this refused line, the Confederates would later build five small forts or "redoubts" along Hillsboro Pike. Finally, Cheatham's corps went in on Lee's right, from near the Franklin Pike to the Nashville & Chattanooga tracks near present-day Polk Avenue. Here, on the eastern end of the Confederate line, they built a strong point, which the Texas troops who manned it named "Granbury's Lunette" in honor of their former commander, Brigadier General Hiram Granbury, killed at Franklin.

Once in place, the Confederate line was over four miles long, and even as thin as it was, it still didn't come close to closing off the city on the south. On the east, there was a two-mile gap from Granbury's Lunette to the Cumberland River above town, with the Murfreesboro and Lebanon Pikes still open. On the west, it was worse. From Stewart's line at the Hillsboro Pike, there was a four-mile gap to the river, which included two major roads leading out of town (Harding and Charlotte Pikes), which were covered only by James Chalmers with about one thousand cavalry. Before the battle, Hood would adjust the center of the main line back south about half a mile so that it lay more along modern-day Woodmont Boulevard. Overall, however, the Confederate position would remain basically unchanged for almost two weeks.

When the Confederates first arrived, the Federal troops—most of them just arrived themselves—expected an attack immediately and worked through the night preparing their positions. In fact, the Confederates had no intention of mounting another assault, and things settled down to the normal action between skirmishers. To the west, however, the Confederates achieved some success. Lieutenant Colonel David Kelley of Chalmers's cavalry moved an artillery battery to Bell's Bend on the Cumberland River and, on the afternoon of December 3, captured two Federal steamers carrying horses and mules. For the next twelve days, Kelley and his detachment managed to block the river below Nashville.[98]

As Hood's army arrived near Nashville, it remained short of almost everything—especially the things that might keep a soldier warm and fed—and its supply line, thin as it was, now stretched over one hundred miles back to the Tennessee River. The soldiers, long accustomed to foraging, fanned out over the countryside in search of food, building materials and firewood. Across the line, the Federal army was much better supplied with most things, but firewood was scarce for it, too. After the armies had been in place about a week, a Federal quartermaster said: "The beautiful woods and groves that surround Nashville…are all going remorselessly down before the axes of the soldiers…If the Rebs coop us up here another fortnight, there won't be a tree left within five miles of Nashville.[99]

Of all the shortages the Confederate suffered, one was particularly serious and persistent. Captain Samuel Foster, Twenty-fourth Texas Cavalry (dismounted)—Cheatham's corps—explained how they managed:

> *We are suffering more for shoes than anything else, and there is no chance to get new ones. At Brigade headquarters, there has been established a shoe shop…they take an old worn out pair of shoes and sew moccasins over them of green cow hide with the hair side in…I am wearing just such foot coverings now, and they are about as pleasant to the foot and about as comfortable as any I ever had.[100]*

On the Federal side, one of the most persistent problems was not with materiel but with pressure from higher headquarters. As soon as word of the results of the Battle of Franklin and Hood's move on to Nashville reached the War Department in Washington and General Grant at City Point, Virginia, everyone from President Lincoln on down began pressuring Thomas to attack Hood immediately. On the morning of December 2, the telegrams began to fly between Washington, City Point and Nashville. The secretary of war made Lincoln's concerns known to General Grant, who then sent two telegrams to Thomas, urging him to "arm and put in the trenches quartermaster employees and citizens if necessary" and then attack Hood before he could fortify. At the end of the same day, Thomas answered with a telegram explaining why he was not yet ready to do that.[101] This type of exchanged would continue for the next five days.

Thomas's reluctance to attack Hood immediately was not because of his infantry strength, which, by December 3, he considered to be adequate, but because of his mounted troops. Most of James Wilson's cavalry units had been campaigning in the field for at least ten days—several of them (Hatch, Croxton and others) for much longer—and were very much in need of remounts and new equipment. Thomas was delaying until he could refit his cavalry for two reasons—one quite sound and one based on faulty intelligence.

Thomas was confident that his infantry could defeat Hood in front of Nashville, but he knew that a strong cavalry force would be vital if he was to finish off Hood's army during the retreat. What Thomas feared was not so

Federal outer defensive line at Nashville, December 15, 1864. *Library of Congress.*

much Hood's army but Nathan Bedford Forrest's cavalry. Such was Forrest's reputation and his success so far in the campaign that both Thomas and James Wilson, his cavalry commander, were convinced that, at the beginning of December, the Confederate cavalry outnumbered the Federal horsemen at least two to one or more. For that reason, Thomas was intent on not only refitting his existing mounted force but also increasing its numbers as much as possible before he committed to an attack.

On December 6, Thomas said that he hoped to have 6,000 to 8,000 cavalry ready in three days and still believed that Forrest had at least 12,000 men to oppose him.[102] In fact, Forrest's entire mounted force never much exceeded 5,000 men during the whole campaign, and at the time Thomas sent his telegram on December 6, estimating Forrest's strength at 12,000, the

Confederate cavalry actually opposing him at Nashville numbered barely 1,000 men (the other 3,500 or so were with Forrest at Murfreesboro or on detached duty elsewhere). Nevertheless, Thomas continued to believe that he was at a serious disadvantage in cavalry.

Finally, on that Tuesday afternoon, after four days of urging, Grant made it a direct order, showing just how big a threat the entire Federal War Department considered Hood's army:

CITY POINT, VA., December 6, 1864—4 p.m.
Major General G.H. THOMAS,
Nashville, Tenn.

Attack Hood at once, and wait no longer for a remount of your cavalry. There is great danger of delay resulting in a campaign back to the Ohio River.

U.S. GRANT,
Lieutenant-General.

Ever the good soldier, Thomas answered five hours later, accepting Grant's order but still complaining that his cavalry force was inadequate:

NASHVILLE, TENN., December 6, 1864—9 p.m.
(Received 12.25 a.m. 7th.)
Lieutenant General U. S. GRANT,
City Point:

Your telegram of 4 p.m. this day is just received. I will make the necessary disposition and attack Hood at once, agreeably to your order, though I believe it will be hazardous with the small force of cavalry now at my service.

GEO. H. THOMAS,
Major-General, U.S. Volunteers, Commanding.[103]

According to the exchange above, the Battle of Nashville should have started on December 7 or early on the eighth at the latest. At this point, however, the weather intervened and delayed things for another week.

By noon of the following day, a cold wind and rain had begun. By the eighth, the rain had turned to sleet and then snow, and that evening, the temperature was down to ten degrees. The next morning, it was six below zero with several inches of ice and snow on the ground, and Thomas's promised attack was delayed.

The bitterly cold weather was hard on everybody, and firewood was scarce everywhere, but at least the Federal troops had huts or tents and blankets. For most of the Confederates, living on the open ground or in shallow holes, the north wind, snow and ice and freezing temperatures were brutal.

> *Edgar Jones, 18th AL*
> *The weather was bitter cold. We were scarce of food and clothing. Many men were still bare-footed, and more becoming so every day. There were no blankets except the ones we carried all summer…I had one, and it had eighteen bullet holes in it.*[104]

> *William Worsham, 19th TN*
> *Ambition, and even life itself, were almost frozen out of us.*[105]

For some, like twenty-five-year-old Sam Watkins of the First Tennessee Infantry, the brutal winter weather only added to the overriding feeling of despair at the condition of the once proud Army of Tennessee:

> *We bivouac on the cold and hard-frozen ground, and when we walk about, the echo of our footsteps sound like the echo of a tombstone. The earth is crusted with snow, and the wind from the northwest is piercing our very bones…Where are our generals? Alas! There are none. Not one single general out of Cheatham's division was left—not one…Nearly all our captains and colonels are gone. Companies mingled with companies, regiments with regiments, and brigades with brigades.*[106]

Hood's army was in no condition to do much other than shelter itself from the cold as best it could. On the west, Stewart tried to work on building the new redoubts along Hillsboro Pike, but the men could not work long in the frigid temperatures, and the ground was frozen.

On the Federal side, inclement weather or not, Ulysses S. Grant, five hundred miles away in Virginia, had run out of patience. By December 9, three days had passed since his direct order to Thomas, and no attack had been made. That morning, Grant had the secretary of war draft an order relieving Thomas of command. Before it was transmitted, however, more information came in from Nashville, and Grant rescinded the order—temporarily—until he could hear further from Thomas.[107] Finally,

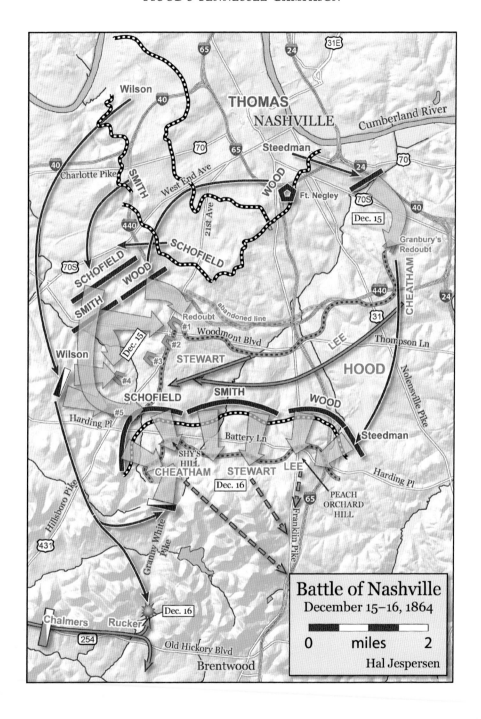

Battle of Nashville
December 15–16, 1864

0 miles 2

Hal Jespersen

on December 13, as the freezing weather dragged on, Grant sent Major General John A. Logan to Nashville to relieve Thomas personally—if he had not attacked Hood by the time Logan arrived. In fact, Logan got no further than Louisville, where he found that the battle was already over on December 17.[108]

Finally, during the night of December 13, the weather changed again, bringing rain and warmer temperatures. One Federal officer observed the next morning:

> *Lt. Thomas C. Thoburn, 50th Ohio*
> *Rain set in during the night and the ice is gone. We now have mud in abundance.*[109]

Confederate crews now set to work in earnest trying to finish the five new redoubts on their western flank, while the Federals were busy getting organized for the attack, which Major General Thomas had ordered to begin at 6:00 a.m. on December 15 "or as soon thereafter as practicable." At 8:00 p.m. that evening, Thomas sent a telegram to Washington assuring Major General Henry Halleck that "the enemy will be attacked tomorrow morning."[110] For both sides at Nashville, the waiting was almost over.

Chapter 9

The Battle of Nashville: The First Day—December 15, 1864

We got orders to be ready to march by 6:00 a.m.[111]
—*William Sthal, Forty-ninth Ohio*

Long before dawn, reveille began to sound throughout the Federal camps as George Thomas's army began to stir. It would be a short winter day with sundown by 4:30 p.m., so Thomas had wanted to start early. His battle plan was not particularly innovative, but its execution would be time consuming and complicated, requiring the movement and coordination of almost fifty thousand men across a front of over seven miles. Thomas planned to begin with a demonstration on the Confederate right near the Murfreesboro Pike and the railroad to Chattanooga, hoping to draw Hood's attention in that direction and prevent those troops from being used to reinforce the Confederate left, where Thomas's real blow would fall.

While his demonstration on the east fixed the Confederate right, Thomas planned to assemble an overwhelming force west of Hillsboro Pike, crush the Confederate left and drive Hood's army back onto the Franklin Pike. That, at least, was the plan. An early morning fog delayed the start of the demonstration on the Confederate right until 8:00 a.m., but then the battle that Grant and the government in Washington had been demanding for almost two weeks got underway.

Major General James B. Steedman had served under George Thomas for most of the war, and on this day, he would begin Thomas's battle at Nashville. Before the war, the forty-seven-year-old Steedman had been a printer and newspaper publisher, a soldier in Texas, a prospector for gold in California and a successful Ohio Democratic politician, supporting Stephen A. Douglas for president in 1860. He raised one of the early ninety-day Ohio regiments (Fourteenth Ohio) and led it in western Virginia. When the Fourteenth reorganized as a three-year regiment, it became part of Thomas's command in Kentucky and moved to Corinth with him after the Battle of Shiloh. Steedman commanded a brigade at Perryville and Stones River and a division at Chickamauga, where he brought reinforcements to George Thomas in time to save his position on Snodgrass Hill.

Steedman had brought three brigades up from Chattanooga two weeks earlier—a total of about 5,200 men. Part of his force, however, was unlike anything many of the other soldiers—Northern or Southern— had ever seen. Two of Steedman's brigades were made up of a total of eight regiments of what Washington

Major General James B. Steedman, commander, Provisional Detachment (District of the Etowah). Steedman brought his Provisional Detachment, which included eight regiments of United States Colored Troops, up from Chattanooga by train. They managed to arrive just before Forrest's cavalry cut the railroad. The USCT performed well and took heavy casualties at Nashville, impressing those who doubted that black soldiers would fight. *Library of Congress.*

had decided to call United States Colored Troops (USCT). Escaped or newly freed slaves and free black men from the North had been enlisting in the Federal army since early 1863, but few Confederates had fought them in the Western Theater. Also, many of the Federal commanders were still not convinced that the black soldiers would fight in the field as well as white troops. At Nashville, George Thomas and many other Federal soldiers would see for themselves.

Steedman started off in the fog at about 6:30 a.m., moving his First and Third Brigades (Morgan and Grosvenor) down the Murfreesboro Pike. By 8:00 a.m., they were in position and began moving west past what they thought was simply a line of empty rifle pits and a "curtain of logs" on their right. In fact, they were moving into a trap. The "curtain of logs" was actually a lunette containing over three hundred men—what remained of Hiram Granbury's brigade—and four artillery pieces. Just behind the lunette, the Nashville & Chattanooga Railroad ran through a twenty-foot-deep cut, blocking any movement across it. Across the railroad cut waited the other two brigades of what had been Patrick Cleburne's division plus a battery of artillery. The Confederates in the little fort watched silently as Colonel Thomas J. Morgan's four USCT regiments marched past them and into what one Southerner called a "perfect slaughter pen."

When the Confederates opened fire on Morgan's USCT troops from two directions, it was devastating. A soldier from Arkansas later said: "The carnage was awful…It is doubtful if a single bullet missed."[112] In the confusion, some of the black troops scrambled down into the railroad cut, where they were shot down by Confederates sealing off the southern end. Morgan was forced to withdraw his four USCT regiments. Lieutenant Colonel Charles H. Grosvenor's brigades of white troops then attacked the lunette head-on but were thrown back with even greater losses. Things soon settled into a stalemate for the rest of the day. Overall, Steedman suffered 250 to 300 casualties. Hood was not fooled by Steedman's attack and did not need to weaken any other part of his line to meet it. His right held firm, and later in the day, he even withdrew most of Cheatham's division and sent them to the left reinforce his crumbling line along Hillsboro Pike. But they arrived too late.

While Steedman's attack was going on, most of the rest of George Thomas's army was in motion, moving into their attack positions. Brigadier General Richard W. Johnson commanded a division of Major General James Wilson's cavalry—almost 2,300 troops. He had been ordered to move out Charlotte Pike and clear the right flank near the Cumberland River. Facing him would be Brigadier General James Chalmers's small Cavalry division—barely 1,000 men. Johnson had planned to get an early start but found the pike blocked by an infantry division and fumed while he was delayed for several hours.

The navy was also active on the Cumberland River that morning, under orders to cooperate with Brigadier General Johnson and finally dislodge Lieutenant Colonel David Kelley and his four guns from their position at Bell's Bend, where they had blocked traffic on the river for almost two weeks. Lieutenant Commander LeRoy Fitch brought seven gunboats down the river and sent the *Neosho* to draw Kelley's fire but then waited all morning for word from Johnson. Later in the afternoon, Fitch closed on Bell's Bend again, as the Federal cavalry approached from the land side, and Kelley was finally forced to withdraw, eventually rejoining Chalmers near Brentwood.[113]

The distance from the Confederate left on Hillsboro Pike to the river to the west was about five miles and had, at first, been the responsibility of Chalmers's division. With his reduced strength, however, this was impossible. So a few days before the battle, a small infantry brigade (Ector's) commanded by Colonel David Coleman was sent to cover the area of Harding Pike (often called Hardin Pike in reports) to Chalmers's right. That morning, at the approach of "a vast body of cavalry and a large brigade of infantry," Coleman pulled his men back toward the main line at Hillsboro Pike without telling Chalmers that his right flank was now uncovered.[114]

Chalmers managed to hold Johnson's division at bay at first but was then forced to retreat two miles when he discovered that his right flank was open. Late in the afternoon, Colonel George Spalding's Twelfth Tennessee Cavalry (U.S.) moved down Harding Pike and captured Chalmers's headquarters wagons, which he had left parked at Belle Meade Plantation. Chalmers's division—two brigades under colonels Edmond Rucker and Jake Biffle—managed to hold Johnson's Federal troops off long enough for David Kelley's detachment and guns to escape from the river at Bell's Bend and then for the division to fall back into the Confederate lines after dark.[115]

As midday approached, the action began to shift to the area of the battlefield along Hillsboro Pike. The center of the Confederate line—from just east of Franklin Pike to Granny White Pike—was held by Lieutenant General S.D. Lee's three divisions. Whether by design or just luck, two of those divisions had seen no real action so far in the campaign, and today would be more of the same. Facing them that morning had been John Schofield's Federal XXIII Corps, but they had been moved to the Federal right to act as reserves for the main attack. Two of Lee's brigades would be moved over to try and shore up A.P. Stewart's crumbling line in the afternoon, but otherwise, Lee's troops would have a relatively easy day.

To S.D. Lee's left, Lieutenant General A.P. Stewart's corps held the left flank of Hood's line. William W. Loring's three brigades stretched from Granny White Pike to Redoubt #1, near Hillsboro Pike. From there, four of Edward C. Walthall's five brigades formed a line at a right angle from Redoubt #1 running south down Hillsboro Pike for almost 1,500 yards. Ector's brigade, as mentioned earlier, had been sent to the west to cover James Chalmers's right flank along Harding Pike but would fall back to the southern end of Walthall's line before the main attack began.[116]

George Thomas's plan to crush the Confederate left meant that his attack would fall almost entirely on A.P. Stewart's line that afternoon. With about 5,000 men, Stewart held a line almost two miles long. Late in the day, Stewart would get about 1,200 more men from Lee's corps to reinforce Walthall's men along Hillsboro Pike, but it was too little and far too late. Against Stewart's position, George Thomas was preparing to bring as many as 35,000 infantry and about 6,000 cavalry.

With all the delays that come with trying to move that many men into position over several miles of ground, it was about 1:00 p.m. before Brigadier General T.J. Wood's IV Corps got Thomas's main attack started. Wood's three divisions were located north and a little west of the angle in Stewart's line at Redoubt #1, but their first objective was an impressive piece of high ground called Montgomery Hill, located about half a mile in front of Loring's line, which faced north along today's Woodmont Boulevard. Soon after they arrived, the Confederates had fortified the hill, so Wood's men were expecting the worst. Unknown to them, however, a few days earlier, Hood had pulled his line back nine hundred yards. At about 1:00 p.m., Brigadier General Samuel Beatty's division made a grand assault up Montgomery Hill only to find it almost abandoned. Wood then began to prepare for the assault on Stewart's line between Granny White and Hillsboro Pike.[117]

Farther to the south, A.J. Smith's XVI Corps was about to become engaged. Smith's corps had marched out of the fortifications that morning into the area between Charlotte Pike and Harding Pike (shown as West End Avenue on the map as it nears town). It marched south and then turned east, crossing Harding Pike, and by early afternoon, John McArthur's division was approaching Redoubt #4 along with some of James Wilson's cavalry who were fighting dismounted. The most westerly placed of the five Confederate strong points, Redoubt #4, sat about two thousand yards southwest of Redoubt #1 and almost one thousand yards in front of Walthall's line of infantry along Hillsboro Pike. Because the cold weather had slowed the work, the small fort was not complete, but was manned by about one hundred Alabama soldiers supporting Captain Charles Lumsden's four-gun artillery battery. About one thousand yards to the south, Redoubt #5 was also manned by about one hundred men plus the crews for two guns.

By 1:30 p.m., the Confederates in Redoubt #4 could see the Federals massing several hundred yards to the west and began an artillery duel with some Federal batteries that lasted about an hour. At about 2:30

p.m., however, the infantry started across the field, and things went quickly. Charles Lumsden and his 150 men had put up a good fight, but they were about to be overwhelmed by Colonel Datus Coon's brigade of dismounted cavalry, followed closely by five regiments from Colonel William McMillen's infantry brigade. As the Federals swarmed over the little redoubt, Captain Lumsden shouted, "Take care of yourselves, boys!" and the surviving Confederates fled across the fields and joined Walthall's men behind a stone wall along Hillsboro Pike.[118]

The Federal cavalrymen who captured Redoubt #4 had no time to celebrate, however, as they immediately came under fire from the two guns of Redoubt #5 to the south. One Iowa cavalryman said that Colonel Coon's five regiments were mixed together, the men following whatever officers happened to be nearby. Under the Confederate fire, they soon decided that it was more dangerous to stay where they were than to advance. As they set off toward Redoubt #5, Sergeant Lyman B. Pierce, Second Iowa Cavalry, said that "the entire brigade was mixed together like a crowd of school boys."[119] Under the assault of Coon's dismounted cavalry, assisted by some of John McArthur's infantry, Redoubt #5 fell in short order.

By late afternoon, Lieutenant General A.P. Stewart's line was in serious trouble. The fall of Redoubts #4 and #5 meant that Major General Edward Walthall's line down the Hillsboro Pike was in imminent danger of being outflanked to the south and overwhelmed from the west. Stewart had already asked for help from S.D. Lee's troops to his right, and the division of Major General Ed Johnson was being pulled out of Lee's line and sent toward Hillsboro Pike, one brigade at a time. Walthall also pulled one of his brigades (Reynolds) out of his already thin line and sent it to shore up his left flank opposite Redoubt #5. There the men found themselves facing a brigade (Hubbard) from John McArthur's division and elements of John Schofield's XXIII Corps that had moved behind A.J. Smith's command and were now crossing the pike just south of Redoubt #5. Even farther south, Ector's small brigade, which had gone into position there after retreating from Harding Pike, had been driven off the pike and up on a hill.

As Reynolds was going into position, the first of the reinforcements from Ed Johnson's division began to arrive on Reynolds's left. Unfortunately, the men of Manigault and Deas's brigades arrived just as several Federal batteries west of the pike opened fire and smothered the Confederate line behind the stone wall with shot and shell. After a few minutes, most of Manigault and Deas's men broke and fell back. The Federal gunners simply elevated their sights a bit and laid another barrage on the Confederates as they broke into the open, causing many of them to return to the stone wall just in time to be overwhelmed by a charge of Federal infantry. Colonel Lucius F. Hubbard's Minnesota and Wisconsin troops routed the two newly arrived brigades, captured about 450 prisoners and crushed the southern end of Walthall's line.[120]

By late in the afternoon, the situation on the Confederate's left flank was accurately described by Lieutenant General A.P. Stewart as "perilous in the extreme." Stewart himself and some other officers had managed to rally some of the survivors from Johnson's two brigades to support some artillery on a hill east of the pike, but they were quickly routed by troops from the XXIII Corps (Couch's division), and the disintegration of Stewart's line continued. To the north, Colonel Sylvester Hill's brigade of McArthur's division stormed Redoubt #3, where Colonel Hill was killed. Under their surviving officers, Hill's brigade then crossed Hillsboro Pike and took Redoubt #2 as well.[121] After the fall of Redoubt #2, Brigadier General Claudius Sears's part of the Confederate line just across the pike was quickly broken, and Sears and his men fell back as best they could. During the retreat, Sears was hit by a random shot. "The ball ricocheted, passed through my poor dear old horse, and crushed my left leg," he later wrote.[122] Finally, as the sun was going down, elements of T.J. Wood's IV Corps stormed Redoubt #1, and the Confederate left flank collapsed.

After two weeks of intense preparation, atrocious weather, prodding and outright threats from higher headquarters, George Thomas had launched his attack. By sundown, he seemed to have every right to feel vindicated. As he received reports of the disintegration of the Confederate left flank, just as he had planned, Thomas might have remembered the telegram he had received six days earlier, when his command of the army seemed to hang by a thread:

CITY POINT, VA., December 9, 1864—7.30 p.m.
Major-General THOMAS,
Nashville, Tenn.:

Your dispatch of 1 p.m. received. I have as much confidence in your conducting a battle rightly as I have in any other officer; but it has seemed to me that you have been slow, and I have had no explanation of affairs to convince me otherwise. Receiving your dispatch of 2 p.m. from General Halleck, before I did the one to me, I telegraphed to suspend the order relieving you until we should near further. I hope most sincerely that there will be no necessity of repeating the orders, **and that the facts will show that you have been right all the time** [author's emphasis].

U.S. GRANT[123]

Now the facts had indeed proved Thomas right, but the next question was: "What will Hood do now?" Will tomorrow bring another fight or the pursuit of a beaten army? One of the Federal senior officers had no doubts. John Schofield had known Hood at West Point, graduating in the same class and, some say, even occasionally tutoring him in mathematics. He had also fought Hood around Atlanta, at Spring Hill and at Franklin. Even with the beating Hood had taken on this day, Schofield was certain that Hood would still be there tomorrow—and he was right.

Chapter 10

The Battle of Nashville:
The Second Day—December 16, 1864

I never saw dead men thicker than in front of my two right regiments.
—Brigadier General James Holtzclaw (CSA) at Peach Orchard Hill[124]

The coming of darkness saved A.P. Stewart's battered corps and might
have prevented the rout of Hood's entire army. George Thomas and his
commanders could certainly be forgiven for believing that the Confederates
were on the verge of collapse and might even retreat during the night. A
closer look at the day's action, however, gives a different picture. In spite of
the beating taken by Stewart's corps, most of the real damage had fallen on
just one of his divisions—Walthall's. His other division—Loring's—escaped
mostly intact except for some lost artillery. Of Hood's other two infantry
corps, Cheatham, on the right, had kept Steedman's troops in check with
very little effort all day. In the center, except for Ed Johnson's two brigades
that went to reinforce Walthall, S.D. Lee's men had hardly been engaged
at all. Of Hood's eight divisions, only one—and half of another—had
been badly hurt. Although battered and outnumbered at least two to one,
Hood's army and its command structure were still intact after the first day
at Nashville.

Not long after dark, Hood had made the decision that the army would
stay and fight another day, but not, obviously, along the same line. During
the night, the Confederates fell back almost two miles and formed their new
line from about today's I-65 at Harding Place stretching west along a line
generally just south of present-day Battery Lane to a high point, then known

as Compton's Hill, about six hundred yards west of Granny White Pike. From there, the line turned south along a line of hill tops for another one thousand yards or so, making Hood's new line just over three miles long.

Because of the first day's battle, the Confederate army's new line was arranged differently. S.D. Lee's corps simply fell back south down Franklin Pike and became the right flank of the army, with his right anchored on a piece of high ground known locally as Peach Orchard Hill. Frank Cheatham's corps, which had held the right flank for almost two weeks, pulled out of its position late in the day, marched behind both Lee and Stewart and, during the night, went into position on the left, beginning at Compton's Hill and running south. A.P. Stewart's battered corps now held the center, with Walthall's division connecting with Cheatham's men at the base of Compton's Hill and running east to Granny White Pike. Loring's division continued east of Granny White Pike until it linked up with Ed Johnson's division of Lee's corps.

Each unit began entrenching the ground in front of its position, but on Compton's Hill, a problem developed that was not discovered until it was too late. Ector's brigade had occupied the hill at the end of the first day and had begun a line of defensive works and rifle pits before it was replaced by Bate's division of Cheatham's corps during the night. In the darkness, Bate's men simply continued the work already started. After dawn, however, it was discovered that the line was too far back from what is known as the "military crest," which meant that an attacking force would be sheltered from the defender's fire by the slope of the hill until they were only a few yards away. During the daylight, Federal snipers and artillery fire kept the defenders pinned down so that they were unable to correct this critical mistake. A few hours later, twenty-six-year-old Lieutenant Colonel William Shy, commanding the Twentieth Tennessee, would die defending the position that was then renamed Shy's Hill in his honor.[125]

As daylight came, William Bate began to take stock of his position on Compton's Hill. To his south, elements of John Brown's and Pat Cleburne's old divisions extended the Confederate line along several hills for about one thousand yards. To the west lay John Schofield's Federal XXIII Corps—about 10,000 men—and to Schofield's right, James Wilson's Federal cavalry was moving around the south end of the Confederate line. By early afternoon, they had outflanked the Confederate left and crossed the Granny White Pike, cutting off the escape route assigned to Cheatham's corps. To the north, Bate could see A.J. Smith's Federal XVI Corps—another 10,000 men—stretching from just opposite his position off to the east. The situation

Lieutenant General Stephen D. Lee, corps commander, Confederate Army of Tennessee. Lee commanded three divisions during the Tennessee Campaign. Of Hood's army, Lee's corps suffered the least during the campaign and provided most of the early rear guard troops during the retreat. *Library of Congress.*

was not encouraging, to say the least. Bate's little division, ordered to hold the critical position on the Confederate left flank, numbered perhaps 1,500 men.[126]

On the opposite end of the Confederate line, S.D. Lee's three divisions were improving their line on the right flank of the army, and their key position was Peach Orchard Hill. Lee had placed the division of Major General Henry D. Clayton on the hill and across Franklin Pike, with the division of Major General Carter L. Stevenson extending the line to the left. There, Major General Ed Johnson's depleted division continued the line to the west until it connected with Stewart's corps. Johnson's division had fought at Franklin and the previous day along the left flank, but Clayton's and Stevenson's troops had marched over one hundred miles from the Tennessee River without seeing any serious action. Opposite their position was the Federal IV Corps commanded by Brigadier General Thomas J. Wood. Lee's corps was currently Hood's strongest unit, fielding about seven thousand men and accounting for at least 40 percent of Hood's infantry at Nashville that morning. T.J. Wood's corps, which they faced, accounted for only about 25 percent of Thomas's infantry but still outnumbered Lee at least two to one, fielding about fourteen thousand men. As Lee's men would shortly prove, however, numbers aren't everything.[127]

Holding the center of Clayton's line on Peach Orchard Hill was Brigadier General James Holtzclaw's brigade. Born in Georgia and raised in Alabama, Holtzclaw had refused an appointment to West Point as a young man and later entered the war as a lieutenant in the Eighteenth Alabama. Now a brigadier general, Holtzclaw and his men would be at the center of the action on this day. They and the brigade of Brigadier General Marcellus Stovall, to their right, would shortly inflict, in half an hour, fully a third of the Federal casualties suffered during the entire two-day battle.

December 16 began in a somber, serious mood. One Confederate remembered that "the morning opened silent and murky." Another said that it was "a gloomy, drizzly dark day; not very cold but foggy, more or less."[128] For the morning and the early afternoon, both sides seemed content to hold their positions, but even though the Federals hadn't yet mounted a major assault, the day was not a quiet one for the Confederates. The Federal army had plenty of artillery and—more importantly—plenty of ammunition, so for several hours, it shelled the Confederate lines.

The Federal IV Corps artillery seemed particularly intense and accurate as they pounded Clayton's division on Peach Orchard Hill. Brigadier General Marcellus Stovall's brigade took the brunt of T.J. Wood's artillery. In his official report, Stovall wrote: "About 9 a.m. on the 16th the enemy planted a battery which completely enfiladed my entire front. During the whole day I was therefore subjected to a fire of artillery, both direct and on my left, quite as severe as any to which I have ever been exposed."[129]

One of Stovall's men wrote in his diary: "The cannonading was terrific and continued almost without intermission during the day…To lie under such a destructive artillery fire produces a feeling of dread that cannot be described. This is more demoralizing than to be actively engaged in battle."[130]

Around noontime, Thomas met with Wood and viewed the IV Corps' position. According to Wood's report, Thomas said that the primary objective was still to turn the Confederate left, but that he (Wood) "should constantly be on the alert for any openings for a more decisive effort." Shortly after noon, Major General Steedman brought his troops up on Wood's left, facing the eastern slopes of Peach Orchard Hill. Soon after Steedman was in place, Wood decided that he had before him one of those "openings for a more decisive effort" that Thomas had mentioned. He would assault Peach Orchard Hill and collapse the Confederate right.

For the effort against the hill, Wood chose the division of Major General Samuel Beatty. Colonel Sidney Post's brigade would make the assault, supported by Colonel Able Streight's brigade. Steedman, to the left, agreed to add Colonel Charles R. Thompson's USCT brigades to the effort as well. The ground in front of the Confederate position was cleared for some distance, so there was no cover for the attackers, and their preparations were in plain sight of the defenders, who waited grimly. To James Holtzclaw's right-hand regiment, the Eighteenth Alabama, there was an added element, as they saw Thompson's USCT brigade. "To our disgust, they were all negroes…That seemed to remove all doubt as to what the result would be."[131]

It was about 3:00 p.m. when Wood gave the order for the assault to begin. The Federal artillery kept up its fire until it became a danger to the approaching troops of Post's brigade, and then they were on their own. Post's skirmish line swept forward until, about thirty yards from the breastworks, a line of brush and sharpened stakes blocked their way. Behind the skirmishers, Post's first line then came up, and the Confederates shot them to pieces. They were followed by a second line and then by three lines from Able Streight's supporting brigade. None of the Federal lines was able to reach the Confederate works. To the left, Steedman's USCT troops were receiving even harsher treatment. In addition to small arms fire, they were raked by canister from a Confederate battery and fire from Stovall's brigade. The battery also punished the left of Post's men and wounded Colonel Post himself. Some of the USCT troops actually veered across the face of the hill in front of Post's men and reached the Confederate breastworks but were all shot down. Another brigade from Steedman's command—white troops under Lieutenant Colonel Charles H. Grosvenor—moved up on the left of the USCT troops but soon broke and ran under the intense fire. James Holtzclaw, commanding the Confederate line in front of Post, Streight and Steedman's troops, later wrote:

> *The enemy made a most determined charge on my right. Placing a negro brigade in front they gallantly dashed up to the abatis, forty feet in front, and were killed by hundreds…they continued to come up in masses to the abatis, but they came only to die. I have seen most of the battle-fields of the West, but never saw dead men thicker than in front of my two right regiments; the great masses and disorder of the enemy enabling the left to rake them in flank, while the right, with a coolness unexampled, scarcely threw away a shot at their front.* [132]

Also watching the attack was a young Federal officer who would later become a well-known author. Thirty-four years later, then First Lieutenant Ambrose Bierce would write about the first time he saw black troops in combat:

> *I was serving on Gen. Beatty's staff, but was not doing duty that day, being disabled by a wound—just sitting in the saddle and looking on. Seeing the darkies going in on our left I was naturally interested and observed*

them closely. Better fighting was never done. The front of the enemy's earthworks was protected by an intricate abatis of felled trees denuded of their foliage and twigs. Through this obstacle a cat would have made slow progress; its passage by troops under fire was hopeless from the first—even the inexperienced black chaps must have known that. They did not hesitate a moment: their long lines swept into that fatal obstruction in perfect order and remained there as long as those of the white veterans on their right. And as many of them in proportion remained until borne away and buried after the action. It was as pretty an example of courage and discipline as one could wish to see. [133]

In spite of the courage and discipline, it was simply too much. The four Federal brigades fell back, leaving their dead and wounded, and it was only "with great difficulty" that the Confederate commanders prevented their jubilant men from climbing over their works and pursuing. T.J. Wood reformed his battered brigades and waited for further developments, which were not long in coming.

Just over two miles to the west, Bate's men on top of Compton's Hill were attracting the attention of the Federal artillery as well. Lieutenant James Cooper, aide to Brigadier General T.B. Smith, said that the shelling began in earnest about noon, with four Federal batteries firing on about two acres of ground on the top of the hill. Because of the fact that Compton's Hill formed a salient, jutting out to the north, Bate said that fire was coming in to his position from three directions, often hitting his troops in the back. Meanwhile, James Wilson's cavalry continued to move around the south end of the Confederate line, and units were pulled out to meet that threat in the rear, thinning the line south of Bate even further.

West and south of Compton's Hill, John Schofield, commanding the Federal XXIII Corps, had been fretting all day, worried that the Confederates might mount an attack on his line, and trying to evaluate reports of Confederates on his southern flank. As he had all through the campaign, Schofield tended to believe the worst and consistently overestimated the enemy's numbers and capabilities. At about 1:30 p.m., Schofield sent a message to Thomas stating, "I have not attempted to advance my main line today and do not think I am strong enough to do so." [134] In fact, Schofield outnumbered the Confederate forces in his front at least two to one and probably more. To the north, however, another commander was thinking differently.

John McArthur was born in Scotland but had moved to Chicago fifteen years earlier. On this day, he was commanding a division in A.J. Smith's XVI

Corps and was positioned just to the north of Compton's Hill. McArthur knew that the hill was the key to the Confederate line, but as the day wore on, he began to fear that no move would be made against it before sundown, allowing the enemy to fortify it further during the night. At about 3:00 p.m., McArthur sent a message to Major General Smith saying that he intended to attack unless orders were received to the contrary. Before any word could get back, McArthur sent two of his brigades forward—McMillen's followed by Hubbard's—under the cover of the division's artillery.

Compton's Hill's north face was very steep, disrupting McMillen's formation as each man had to take his own route to the top, climbing as best he could. McMillen's right and center regiments were somewhat shielded from enemy fire as they climbed, but the Tenth Minnesota, on his left, was punished by fire from Confederates of Walthall's division between the hill and Granny White Pike. Even more exposed was Hubbard's brigade, which followed closely behind and to McMillen's left. As they slogged across a muddy field, Walthall's men fired into them from the front, and one of Loring's batteries from across the pike raked their left flank. One of Hubbard's regiments, the Fifth Minnesota, lost four color-bearers and suffered 25 percent casualties, but Hubbard's men carried the line held by Walthall's division to the right of Compton's Hill.

While Hubbard's men fought through the muddy cornfield, McMillen's men gained the top of Compton's Hill and quickly engaged Finley's and T.B. Smith's small brigades. The fight was short but vicious. Lieutenant Colonel Shy and a small group fought to the end, with Shy being shot in the head at close range. Major General Bate, being mounted, barely escaped down the hill, while Brigadier General Thomas Benton Smith was captured. As he was being led away as a prisoner, a Federal officer struck Smith several times on the head with a saber, fracturing his skull. The doctors expected the wound to be fatal, but Smith recovered and lived another fifty-nine years. He suffered brain damage, however, and spent his last forty-seven years in a mental institution.[135]

George Thomas had ridden over to Schofield's headquarters when McArthur's attack began. Seeing the Federal troops going up Compton's Hill, Thomas ordered Schofield to attack as well. Within moments, one of Brigadier General Jacob Cox's brigades under Colonel Charles C. Doolittle surged up the hills in their front and routed the men of John Brown's old division, who were now outflanked on their right due to the fall of Compton's Hill. In what seemed like only minutes, the Confederate left flank, held by Frank Cheatham's corps, began to fall apart. The troops were stretched so thin that there were no reserves to send in, and once broken, the line was quickly crushed like an egg shell as McArthur's success on Compton's Hill became contagious and more and more Federal units advanced.

As unit cohesion broke down, the Confederate retreat quickly became one of small groups and individuals. Cheatham's corps was supposed to retreat by way of the Granny White Pike, but by now, it was blocked by Federal cavalry. The only way out was to keep going across the pike, climb the Overton Hills and try to gain the Franklin Pike near Brentwood. For most of these already exhausted men, that would mean a trek of more than three miles. With no roads over the hills, almost all the wheeled vehicles and artillery that couldn't make it to the Franklin Pike were lost.

To the east of Compton's Hill, the disintegration of the Confederate line continued. Once Hubbard's Federal brigade broke Walthall's line between Compton's Hill and Granny White Pike, some of them turned to their left and began to fire into the flank of Loring's division across the pike. As other Federal units saw what was happening, some began to attack the Confederate line head-on while others worked around to the flank and rear, forcing one Confederate regiment after another out of their position and sending them fleeing over the hills in their rear toward the Franklin Pike. In this way, the Federal infantry began to roll up the Confederate line from west to east.

Before long, Loring's division also fell back, joining the exodus over the hills toward Brentwood, and the Federal onslaught fell on S.D. Lee's left division, commanded by Major General Ed Johnson. In his official report, Lee described the scene as his men, still celebrating their own victory against the Federal attack on Peach Orchard Hill, realized what had happened in the center of the Confederate line:

> *The troops of my entire line were in fine spirits and confident of success—so much so that the men could scarcely be prevented from leaving their trenches to follow the enemy on and near the Franklin pike; but suddenly all eyes were turned to the center of our line of battle near the Granny White pike…Our men were flying to the rear in the wildest confusion, and the enemy following with enthusiastic cheers. The enemy at once closed toward the gap in our line and commenced charging on the left division (Johnson's) of my corps…The enemy soon gained our rear, and was moving on my left flank, when my line gradually gave way. My troops left their line in some disorder, but were soon rallied and presented a good front to the enemy. It was a fortunate circumstance that the enemy was too much crippled to pursue us on the Franklin pike.*[136]

Being on the eastern end of the line, S.D. Lee had been able to see the disaster coming and therefore had a little warning. It was not enough to save Ed Johnson's division (Major General Johnson himself was captured along with many of his men), but it was enough to get his remaining two divisions moving back in some semblance of order. In front of Lee's corps, T.J. Wood's IV Corps, fresh from its repulse at Peach Orchard Hill, saw what was happening and began to press forward as well. Lee was able to rally some of his men and set up a blocking force on Franklin Pike that managed to delay Wood's IV Corps north of Brentwood until darkness ended their pursuit. S.D. Lee and his hastily assembled force was one of two units that kept the Confederate retreat, as chaotic as it was, from turning into a full-blown rout. As Lee continues in his report: "The only pursuit made at that time was by a small force coming from the Granny White pike." Sent to meet this threat was the small cavalry brigade of Colonel Edmond Rucker.

During the two-day Battle of Nashville, the only cavalry asset General Hood had available on the battlefield was the division commanded by Brigadier General James Chalmers—about 1,200 men. On the first day of the battle (the fifteenth), Chalmers had fallen back from his position on the far Confederate left near the Cumberland River to the Hillsboro Pike. On the second day (the sixteenth), Chalmers continued to fall back until, late in the afternoon, "the whole brigade…was formed in front of Brentwood, to protect the wagons and ambulances which were collected there." It was there, at about 4:30 p.m., that he got an order from Hood to "hold the Granny White pike at all hazards." Colonel Edmund Rucker's brigade was then sent back about a mile and a half to the pike and blocked it about five hundred yards north of the present-day intersection of Granny White and Old Hickory Boulevard.[137]

During the day on the sixteenth, the Federal cavalry division under Edward Hatch had moved around the southern end of the Confederate line and managed to block the Granny White Pike, which was supposed to be Cheatham's corps' escape route. When the Confederate line broke, Cheatham's men were forced to flee overland to the east, across the Overton Hills, and Hatch's men, who had been fighting dismounted all day, were then ordered to bring up the horses and start down the Granny White Pike to intercept the retreating Confederate column along Franklin Pike. According to James Wilson's report, "Hatch was ordered to mount his division and press rapidly down the Granny White pike for the purpose of striking the enemy again at or beyond Brentwood." He had not proceeded far before he encountered Chalmers's division of cavalry.[138]

The engagement that followed came to be known as the "Battle of the Barricades." Major General James Wilson later described it as "one of the most exciting of the war." During the fight, two of the senior officers supposedly met on the battlefield. Colonel Rucker, coming upon some mounted troops in the dark, asked, "Who are you anyway?" Colonel George Spalding replied that he was the commander of the Twelfth Tennessee Cavalry (U.S.). Rucker grabbed the reins of Spalding's horse and replied that he was the commander of the Twelfth Tennessee Rebel Cavalry and that Spalding was his prisoner. Spalding replied, "Not by a damn sight" and then jerked his horse away. Moments later, another officer shot Rucker in the arm, and it was the Rebel colonel who became a prisoner.[139] The outnumbered Confederates managed to hold the pike until almost midnight and then fell back to join the retreat. By their stubborn resistance on Granny White Pike, Rucker's men ended the Federal army's last chance to disrupt the Confederate retreat that night.

Somehow, in all the confusion, General Hood had managed to dispatch a staff officer to Forrest at Murfreesboro with orders for him to fall back. One of his divisions (Buford's) was sent to Franklin to help protect the withdrawal while Forrest began moving the rest of his command south, with orders to meet the army at Pulaski. On the way, Forrest would change his destination to Columbia, which would prove fortunate for Hood and the army.[140]

Chapter 11

The Retreat—Nashville to Columbia

The rout and retreat were inevitable…the only wonder is that he [Thomas] *did not capture us all.*
—Capt W.O. Dodd, Chalmers's division, CSA cavalry[141]

The Confederate Army of Tennessee had been through a lot in its two-year life. Just in the last three and a half weeks, it had endured the rigors of the march from the Tennessee River, the bitter disappointment of the missed opportunity at Spring Hill, the bloody debacle at Franklin and the privations of living out in the open during the Tennessee winter. Even after the collapse of the left flank the day before, it still began on this day, ragged and outnumbered as it was, as a functioning army. When darkness came, however, there was the real feeling, from the privates through the generals, that something within the army had finally been broken.

On the evening of the sixteenth, an officer in a South Carolina regiment described the scene in the little village of Brentwood as "bedlam." Two of the survivors of the fight on Compton's Hill (now Shy's Hill) later described what they found when they made it to the pike:

Night closed down on a thoroughly demoralized and routed mob making all possible haste to get into the Franklin Pike before their only way of retreat should be blocked. James Cooper, aide to Brigadier General T.B. Smith

We saw demoralization in the extreme. Riding down the pike about a mile, we saw Gen. Hood with other commanding officers, trying to rally the men, but in vain. Charles B. Martin, 1ˢᵗ Georgia Volunteers[142]

A Tennessee soldier described what he saw:

Hood's whole army was routed and in full retreat…General Frank Cheatham and General William B. Bate tried to form a line at Brentwood, but the line they formed was like trying to stop the current of the Duck River with a fish net. Sam Watkins, 1ˢᵗ Tennessee infantry.[143]

While that night it might have looked to the average soldier, like those above, that the army was broken beyond repair, there were still units that retained their organization, and officers were already preparing for what was to come. The rear guard actions on the Franklin and Granny White Pikes had bought Hood's army a few hours, but that was all. None doubted that the Federal pursuit would begin at first light. There were plans to be made and things to be done if the army was to survive.

At George Thomas's headquarters, the congratulations were coming in from many of the same people who, a few days ago, were calling for him to be relieved. Even with the congratulations, however, came reminders that the job was not finished:

WASHINGTON, D.C., December 16, 1864.
(Sent 11:25 a.m.)
Major-General THOMAS,
Nashville, Tenn.:

Please accept for yourself, officers, and men the nation's thanks for your good work of yesterday. You made a magnificent beginning. A grand consummation is within your easy reach. Do not let it slip.

A. LINCOLN.[144]

Thomas, of course, had no intention of letting it slip, and it was now that Thomas's insistence on remounting and refitting his cavalry would begin to pay dividends. Major General James Wilson began the battle with at least eight thousand Federal cavalry, and on the morning of the seventeenth, he would have them all on the road in pursuit of Hood's army. Wilson sent

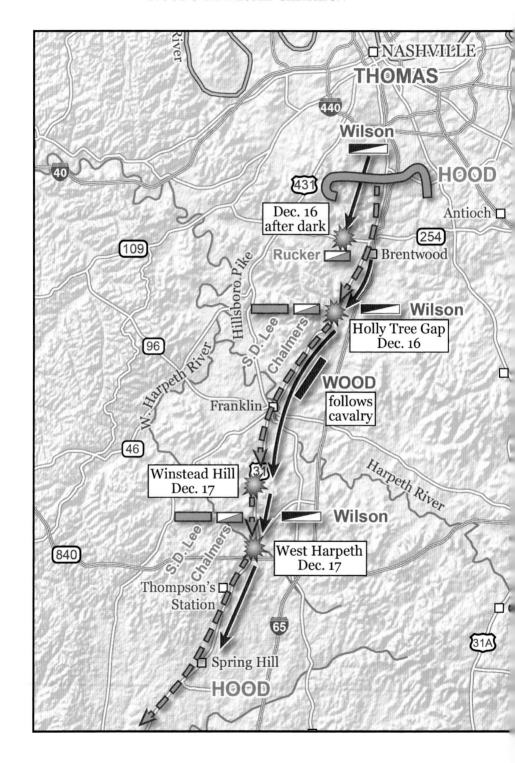

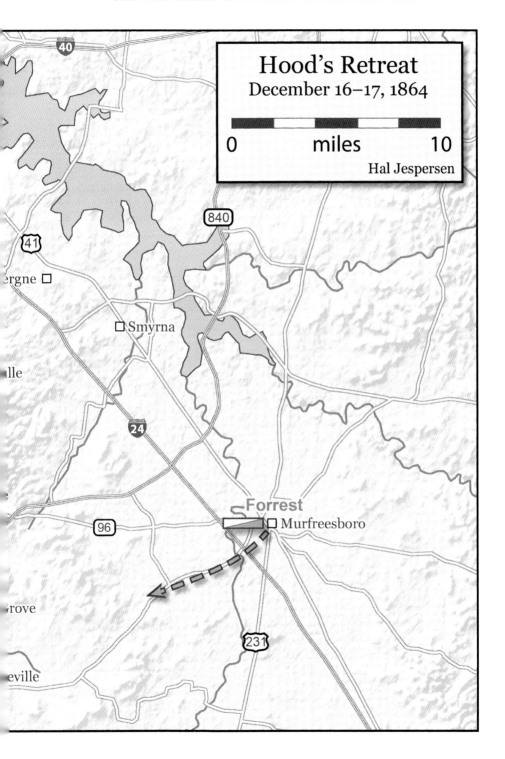

Hood's Retreat
December 16–17, 1864

0 miles 10

Hal Jespersen

Brigadier General Richard Johnson's division down the Hillsboro Pike to try to cut off the Confederate column at Franklin. Wilson knew that his main adversary would be the enemy cavalry under James Chalmers, and he told Johnson, "Shove him as closely as possible; give him no peace. A dispatch from General Hood, captured with General Rucker, says the safety of his army depends upon the ability of Chalmers to keep us off; time is all he wants. Don't give him any."[145]

Wilson then moved from Granny White over to the Franklin Pike, sent a brigade under John Croxton down the Wilson Pike to the east and then set off after the rear of the Confederate column with his main force. He soon found them, but it was infantry in addition to Rebel horsemen.

About four miles down the road toward Franklin, the Confederates were getting into position for the first of many rear guard actions. Major General Henry D. Clayton's division had remained relatively intact and now set up a blocking position in a small pass through a range of hills that is today called Holly Tree Gap (usually called Hollow Tree Gap in reports). In addition to his three brigades, he had managed to stop one of Stevenson's as well (Pettus). Clayton had also attached one of Frank Cheatham's passing artillery batteries and so had a respectable force to hold the little pass.[146] One Confederate officer later wrote, "A good many soldiers had come in through the night and early hours of the 17th, so that it looked more like an army again."[147]

Some Confederate cavalry had moved back up the pike toward Brentwood, but by 8:00 a.m., Wilson's advancing troops were pushing them back with ease until they came to Clayton's troops posted at Holly Tree Gap. The Confederate riders dashed to the rear "in a most shameful manner," according to Clayton, but the Federal riders were turned back by the line of infantry.[148] Clayton and his men held the gap for about two hours but then began to fall back toward Franklin, closely pursued by Brigadier General John Hammond's brigade of Brigadier General Joseph Knipe's division. Reaching the Harpeth River just before noon, Gibson's and Pettus's brigades, along with some of Buford's cavalry, were left to cover a temporary pontoon bridge while the rest of Lee's command crossed. They were soon attacked by Hammond's brigade, and a sharp fight commenced on the north bank of the Harpeth and on the grounds of today's Harlinsdale Farms. Most of the rear guard managed to escape, covered by some artillery in the town, before the pontoons were sunk, but they still lost over one hundred men.

With all his troops across the river, S.D. Lee continued to fall back. Franklin was still full of sick and wounded men from the fight two weeks earlier, and Lee had no desire to see the town become a battlefield. Also, an hour or so earlier, R.W. Johnson's Federal cavalry division had crossed the river on Hillsboro Pike a couple miles to the west and were now on the south side of the Harpeth. With Knipe's men threatening from the north and Johnson to the west, Lee's rear guard was in danger of being cut off from the rest of the army and caught between the two Federal forces. Before leaving Franklin, however, a party under Captain Coleman, an engineer on Lee's staff, managed to drop the railroad bridge, which delayed Knipe's cavalry several hours but would prove much more of an obstacle once the Federal infantry arrived.

Early in the afternoon, James Wilson sent a message to headquarters from Franklin:

> *HDQRS. CAVALRY CORPS, MIL. DIV. OF THE MISSISSIPPI,*
> *Franklin, Tenn., December 17, 1864—1 p.m.*
> *Brigadier General W.D. WHIPPLE,*
> *Chief of Staff, Department of the Cumberland:*
>
> *GENERAL: The rebels are on a great skedaddle; the last of them, closely pressed by Knipe, passed through this place two hours and a half ago.*[149]

During the rest of the afternoon on December 17, S.D. Lee's hastily assembled rear guard would fight two more sharp engagements. The first occurred where the Columbia Pike crossed a ridgeline at Winstead Hill, about three miles south of downtown Franklin, and near the site of General Hood's command post during the battle of November 30. In this engagement, Lee was wounded but remained in command, and the Federal pursuit was delayed even more. Lee estimated that between this action and the destruction of the railroad bridge, he managed to buy four to five more hours for the retreating army.[150]

The last rear guard action—and the most vicious—took place just over six miles south of Franklin. Lieutenant General Lee, being wounded in the foot, had moved on toward Spring Hill and left the rear guard in the hands of Major General Carter L. Stevenson, who, with about seven hundred men and some cavalry, formed a line across the pike near the West Harpeth River at about 4:00 p.m. It was within an hour of sunset when Federal cavalry under James Wilson arrived with elements of Edward Hatch and Joseph Knipe's divisions and their artillery—possibly as many as five thousand men. Against such odds, Stevenson's rear guard was in a tight spot.

In the cold drizzle and fog and the failing light, troops on both sides had difficulty telling friend from foe. Also, according to Stevenson, early on in the engagement, he "found it impossible to control the cavalry and…get them into action." Soon Wilson's men were flowing around both flanks of Stevenson's position, and he was forced to conduct a fighting withdrawal back across the West Harpeth. In spite of what Stevenson thought, the Confederate cavalry was fighting, too, with both Brigadier General Chalmers and the newly arrived Brigadier General Abraham Buford involved in hand-to-hand combat with the enemy in the approaching darkness. Soon Stevenson was pressed again and had to continue falling back, but he finally received some support. Major General Clayton's and his division were a short distance to the south on their way to Spring Hill when he heard the fighting begin behind him. Fearing that Stevenson was in trouble, Clayton sent some troops back to help. Together, Clayton and Stevenson's troops were able to fend off the last of the Federal attacks and eventually fall back to Spring Hill, where the main body of the Confederate army bivouacked for the night.[151]

So far, the pursuit had been an all-Federal cavalry affair. Brigadier General T.J. Wood and his IV Corps had started out down the Franklin Pike early in the morning and arrived on the north bank of the Harpeth River at Franklin by early afternoon, but by then, the action had already moved south of town. More importantly, there was no bridge at Franklin, and the river was rising. Wood sent word back for Thomas to hurry the pontoon train and set some of his engineers to work trying to rig some kind of a bridge in the meantime. Working through the night in the rising river, Colonel Isaac Suman and men of the Ninth Indiana managed to get a workable bridge in place, and Wood's corps began crossing at about 7:30 on Sunday morning, December 18.[152] S.D. Lee's destruction of the bridges at Franklin had delayed the Federal infantry for eighteen hours, with them finally crossing the river without the aid of pontoons. The pontoon train was still desperately needed, however, which is another story altogether.

Chapter 12

The Retreat—Columbia to the Tennessee River

They are the worst looking and most broken down looking set I ever laid eyes on.
—resident of Columbia, Tennessee, December 20, 1864[153]

With two major rivers and many smaller streams to cross, all swollen by the recent rains, pontoons to construct temporary bridges for the Federal army and its heavy equipment were vital to the pursuit of the Confederates. Accordingly, General Thomas issued the following order to the officer in charge of the pontoon train:

> *HEADQUARTERS DEPARTMENT OF THE CUMBERLAND,*
> *OFFICE CHIEF ENGINEER, Nashville, Tenn., December 16, 1864.*
> *Major JAMES R. WILLETT, First U.S. Veteran Volunteer Engineers, &c.:*
>
> *SIR: In accordance with instructions received from the major-general commanding the department, you will move the pontoon train at as early an hour as possible, on the Murfreesborough pike, being prepared to report with it to the commanding general at any point between Brentwood and Columbia. As soon as this is done you will report to him in person for special instructions.*
>
> *I am, very respectfully, your obedient servant,*
> *H.C. WHARTON,*
> *Lieutenant Colonel and Chief of Engineers, Dept. of the Cumberland.*

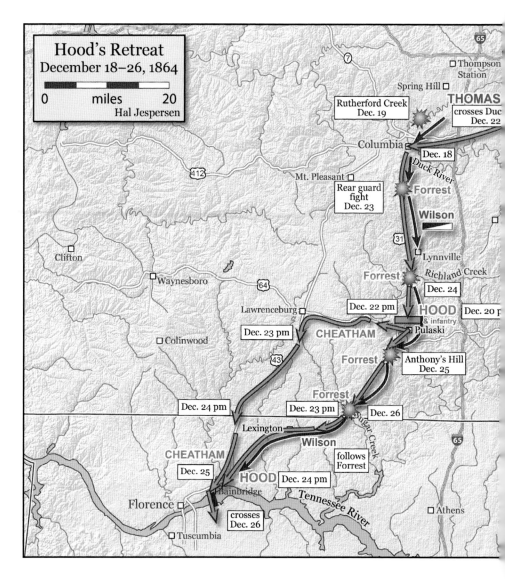

Following his orders, Major Willett got the wagon train, pulled by five hundred mules, on the road the next morning and marched fifteen miles toward Murfreesboro before it was discovered that they were going in the wrong direction. The order should have said "the Franklin Pike." After a day's march, the pontoons were farther from where they were needed than if they had simply sat all day in Nashville! There was nothing to do but turn around and head back and start again on the correct road. The pontoon train finally crossed the Harpeth at Franklin on the morning of the twentieth.

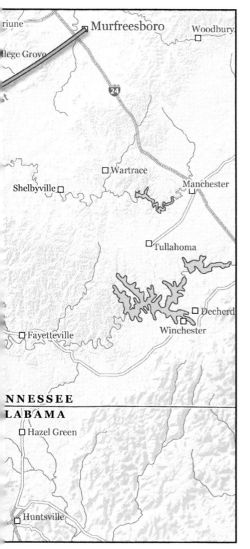

By that time, the IV Corps infantry was almost twenty miles to the south and just beginning to cross Rutherford Creek on makeshift footbridges. The journal of the Fourth Army Corps estimated that the lack of pontoons at Franklin and Rutherford Creek delayed them "about three days."[154]

T.J. Wood's IV Corps had crossed the Harpeth River at Franklin on the morning of the eighteenth and camped about three miles south of Spring Hill that evening. A.J. Smith's XVI Corps crossed the Harpeth that same day and camped just south of Franklin. A.J. Smith's XVI Corps would follow Wood's IV Corps during the rest of the pursuit, but none of Smith's infantry would get close enough to engage in any of the rear guard actions. Further south at Columbia, the Confederate army began crossing the Duck River on the eighteenth, with Hood setting up his headquarters there in a private home. Finally, during the evening, Forrest arrived, having moved most of his command from Murfreesboro in a two-day forced march.

On the morning of the nineteenth, the leading elements of Wilson's cavalry and Wood's IV Corps reached the north bank of Rutherford Creek, less than four miles from Columbia. Forrest's newly arrived men joined Cheatham's men, who had destroyed the wagon and railroad bridges and were posted on the bluffs on the south bank. They were ordered to pull back that afternoon. Even with the Confederates gone from the south bank, however, the Federals were still stuck. The rains had swollen Rutherford Creek so that it was fifteen feet deep at the fords. With the pontoon train miles in the rear, Wood's men worked through the frigid night to build footbridges and began crossing the next morning.[155]

On the night of the nineteenth, Hood and Forrest met in Columbia to decide the fate of the army. According to Forrest, Hood was afraid that the army could not retreat any further in its broken-down condition, given the severe weather conditions. Forrest, however, believed that to stay where they were meant sure capture, and he offered to cover the retreat of the army to the Tennessee River if his cavalry were reinforced with some infantry units. Hood agreed, and the main body of Hood's army began leaving on the seventy-mile trek the following morning (the twentieth). For the rear guard, Forrest had about 3,000 cavalry left and had requested that he also be given Major General Edward Walthall and 4,000 infantry. What he got was Walthall and about 1,900 men. At least 300 of them were immediately deemed "unserviceable" for lack of shoes and sent with the wagon train. In the end, Forrest and Walthall would have about 4,600 men and eight artillery pieces to hold back Thomas's army.[156]

By the end of December 20, the head of the Confederate column was within three miles of Pulaski, having covered almost thirty miles in the rain that now changed to sleet and snow. Forrest remained in Columbia with his new command and watched as the leading elements of Wood's IV Corps and Wilson's cavalry arrived on the north bank of the Duck River early in the afternoon. George Thomas arrived at Rutherford Creek that evening, and the long-delayed pontoon train camped for the night just south of Spring Hill.

On December 21, the wretched weather continued, punishing both the Northern and Southern armies. The bulk of the Confederate army was in and around Pulaski, Tennessee, and would spend the day combing the countryside in a desperate search for food for the men and forage for the animals. The Federal army was also short of supplies. Since the railroad bridge in Franklin was not yet back in operation, no trains could reach them yet. Wood's Federal IV Corps remained on the north bank of the Duck River, watched by a few Confederate pickets on the south side. Early in the afternoon, the pontoon train finally reached Rutherford Creek, and parts of it were sent forward to the Duck River.

Early on December 22, the Fifty-first Indiana of the IV Corps crossed the Duck River in boats and drove away the Confederate pickets. Work then commenced on the pontoon bridge, which was finished by 6:30 p.m. Wood's IV Corps began to cross immediately and continued through the night even though the IV Corps records stated that "the bridge is in such a bad condition and the descent and ascent of the banks so slippery that it is most difficult to get on and off."[157] As the IV Corps began to cross the river that morning, Forrest and the cavalry fell back a few miles down the Pulaski Pike. Farther south at Pulaski, after a day of rest and foraging, the main body of Hood's army was on the move again. As bad as the turnpike from Columbia had been, the roads from now on would be worse. In order to move faster, Hood decided to split the army, with Frank Cheatham's corps marching west out the road to Lawrenceburg and then turning south to the Tennessee River. General Hood and the main body would take the smaller but more direct Lamb's Ferry Road. There was still forty more miles to go. By the evening of the twenty-second, Cheatham's corps was camped on the Lawrenceburg Road at Richland Creek—just west of Pulaski—and the head of Hood's column was eight miles southwest of Pulaski.[158]

By 5:00 a.m. on December 23, much of Wood's IV Corps infantry was over the Duck River, but they were then forced to give up the pontoon bridge to Wilson's cavalry. At about 2:30 p.m., with the cavalry still crossing, Wood's infantry was ordered to march on out of town a few miles down the Pulaski Pike and go into camp. Just over three miles south of town, some of Wilson's cavalry, moving ahead of the infantry, ran into Forrest's pickets near Beechwood, the home of Major Amos Warfield. Forrest then fell back to his first blocking position. The Federal infantry moved forward and deployed three regiments, which engaged Forrest until darkness closed the action.[159] The day before, Major General Walthall and the Confederate infantry had been ordered back to near Lynnville, so this action involved only Forrest and the cavalry and would be the only rear guard action involving Federal infantry. One of Walthall's officers later wrote of the retreat that "the sufferings of the troops were terrible."[160] Farther south, the Confederate main body crossed the state line and camped for the night four miles from Lexington, Alabama. Cheatham's corps had reached Lawrenceburg and camped a few miles south of town.[161]

On the morning of December 24, James Wilson's cavalry, having finally made it across the pontoon bridge, took the lead in the pursuit down Pulaski Pike. Forrest, in the meantime, had sent Walthall and the infantry farther back to Richland Creek to prepare a defensive position. Forrest then took the cavalry back north on the pike and soon collided with one of Wilson's Federal cavalry units under John Croxton. Throughout the rest of the day, the running cavalry fight, which Forrest called "a severe engagement," fell back south through the little village of Lynnville toward Walthall's position on Richland Creek. Late in the day, there was a rather sharp engagement between the Federal troops of John Croxton and Edward Hatch and Forrest and Walthall's men at Richland Creek. Brigadier General Abraham Buford (CSA) was wounded, and Forrest fell back to Pulaski after dark, but the Confederates were not able to destroy the pike bridge over the creek.[162] To the south, the main body of Hood's army camped that Christmas Eve at Shoal Creek, about two miles from the planned crossing point at Bainbridge, and Cheatham's corps was just across the state line—still half a day's march from the main body. At the river, Hood's engineers were already busy working on a pontoon bridge of their own. The problem was that the pontoon train they had managed to haul down to the river might not have enough boats to stretch across the wide Tennessee River. One officer remembered: "Every mind was haunted by the apprehension that we did not have boats enough to make a bridge...When we left the pike at Pulaski we had an awful road, strewn with dead horses and mules, broken wagons, and worse than all, broken pontoons."[163]

Sometime earlier, Hood had sent a small engineer detachment under Captain Robert Cobb to try and float some captured pontoons down from Decatur, almost forty miles away, but nobody knew yet if Cobb had been successful.

On Christmas morning, December 25, both the Confederate and Federal cavalry were up early—Forrest in the town of Pulaski and Wilson at Richland Creek, about ten miles away. Forrest sent Brigadier General William H. "Red" Jackson's division out to defend the town and sent Walthall's infantry south, down Lamb's Ferry Road, while he stayed in town and tried to destroy as much of the military supplies as he could. These included ammunition and a railroad locomotive. By 8:30 a.m., however, the Fifth Iowa cavalry was pushing Jackson's men back into Pulaski. The Confederates fired the bridge on the south edge of town and made their escape, but Wilson's men put the fire out and soon followed. James Wilson sounded quite confident in the following message, sent that morning:

> *HDQRS. CAVALRY CORPS, MILITARY OF THE MISSISSIPPI,*
> *Pulaski, December 25, 1864—9.10 a.m.*
> *My advance, Colonel Harrison commanding, drove the rebels through this place half past 8 on the keen jump. Forrest, with Jackson's and Buford's divisions, is scarcely out of sight...They are trying to reach Florence. I will crowd them ahead as fast as possible. They are literally running away, making no defense whatever.[164]*

Wilson and the Federal cavalry left Pulaski at about 1:00 p.m., following Forrest on Lamb's Ferry Road, with Wood's infantry following an hour or so later. About seven miles south of Pulaski, however, Wilson's cavalry found out that Forrest was retreating—but he wasn't exactly running away.

After leaving Pulaski in a hurry, Forrest decided to turn on his pursuers, and the place he picked was called Anthony's Hill. He put most of Walthall's men, his cavalry and his artillery out of sight, leaving what looked like a ragged skirmish line in view. The lead regiments of Wilson's force encountered the thin line, quickly pushed them up the hill and walked right into Forrest's ambush. His infantry and artillery opened up, and the enemy broke and fled back down the road, chased by several hundred Confederates, who also managed to capture a piece of artillery. According to Brigadier General Lawrence "Sul" Ross, this "administered such an effectual check that he [the enemy] did not again show himself that day. This done, we retired leisurely, and after night bivouacked on Sugar Creek."[165] Later, the Federal infantry came up to Anthony's Hill and went into camp, waiting for rations.

By now, the main body of Hood's army had arrived at the Tennessee River at Bainbridge. Stewart's corps had set up a defensive line along Shoal Creek, and Cheatham's corps had arrived on the Lawrenceburg Road and gone into a defensive position along with Lee's corps (now commanded by Carter L. Stevenson) guarding the pontoon bridge, which was under construction. As a fine Christmas present for Hood and the army, Captain Cobb arrived with the pontoons from Decatur—to the cheers of the troops—and it was now certain that the bridge would reach across to the south bank.

By dawn on December 26, the Confederate engineers had worked through the night and gotten the pontoon bridge—laid across eighty boats—in operation. S.D. Lee's corps was the first to cross, followed by Frank Cheatham's corps later in the day. A.P. Stewart's corps crossed during the day on the twenty-seventh. Now that they were vulnerable on the river, everyone was worried about the Federal gunboats. Admiral S.P. Lee (USN) had, in fact, been shelling Florence and other targets several miles downriver but could not bring his gunboats over the Muscle Shoals to get in range of the pontoon bridge.[166] Meanwhile, early that morning and twenty-five miles to the north, Nathan Bedford Forrest and his exhausted men prepared for one last meeting with James Wilson's Federal cavalry.

After the fight at Anthony's Hill, Brigadier General "Sul" Ross said that they "retired leisurely," but the truth was actually much bleaker. Forrest's men retired after dark and walked over ten miles back to Sugar Creek under some of the worst conditions imaginable. The country road had already been traveled by the greater part of Hood's army—thousands of men and animals and wagons—and was now a frozen swamp. Some of Forrest's men later said:

The roads were now as bad as ever an army encountered, and the horses had to be pushed through mud and slush every step of the way, often belly deep and never less than up to their knees. The men marched, barefoot in many cases, often waist deep in ice cold water while sleet beat upon their head and shoulders.

Reaching Sugar Creek at about 1:00 a.m., the exhausted troops were allowed to wash the grime off in the creek, start fires and rest for a few hours.[167]

When Forrest arrived at Sugar Creek, the last of the army ordnance wagons were still there, their teams having been used to move the pontoons down to the river. The animals had returned, but Forrest would have to hold the Federals at the creek long enough to give the wagons a head start, so he prepared another ambush. This time, he was helped by the weather as a dense fog settled in about dawn. Just after 8:00 a.m., the leading elements of Wilson's troops began to push the Confederate pickets back cautiously through the fog, crossing the creek and approaching within about thirty yards of the Confederate line. Walthall's infantry opened fire, Forrest's cavalry swept in from both flanks and Wilson's men fled in panic. One source says that Forrest's men chased the Federal troops for a mile before returning to the creek. Forrest said that they captured at least one hundred prisoners, 150 horses and, more importantly, many blue overcoats that the men desperately needed.[168]

The Confederate infantry stayed at Sugar Creek until noon and then started for the river, with Forrest's cavalry following an hour later. Sugar Creek would be the last engagement for Forrest's rear guard and the last combat for the Army of Tennessee in the state. Wilson did not follow for the rest of the day, and Wood's IV Corps infantry remained at Anthony's Hill. That night, James Wilson made one last effort to catch Forrest before he escaped across the Tennessee River. He assembled a five-hundred-man unit of his best mounted men, mostly from Edward Hatch's division, to go forward and try to overtake Forrest. Led by Colonel George Spalding of the Twelfth Tennessee Cavalry (U.S.), they started early the next morning.

Ed Walthall and the Confederate infantry camped for the night of the twenty-sixth near Lexington, Alabama, and moved out early on the twenty-seventh, reaching Shoal Creek by noon. George Spalding's special unit, George Thomas's last chance to catch any of Hood's army north of the Tennessee River, rode through Lexington that afternoon with the rest of Edward Hatch's division a few miles behind. They were still at least fifteen miles from the Confederate defenses at Shoal Creek and seventeen miles from the pontoon bridge, where A.P. Stewart's corps was now crossing.

About midnight, Forrest began to cross his cavalry, the bridge being so treacherous that they had to cross on foot, leading the horses.

By daybreak on the twenty-eighth, Walthall's infantry, the last of the rear guard, had started across, with Ector's brigade bringing up the rear. As soon as Ector's men were clear, Lieutenant Colonel Stephen W. Presstman, the army's acting chief engineer, ordered his men to cut the bridge loose from the north shore. The first Federal unit on the scene—Colonel Spalding's special cavalry group—arrived in time to see the pontoons swinging to the south bank. A Confederate officer later wrote to his wife: "Every wagon, every horse, every mule, the hogs, beeves, cavalry, infantry, and finally, every scout had crossed over."[169]

There, on the banks of the Tennessee River, John Bell Hood's Tennessee Campaign, the last offensive mounted by the Confederacy, ended where it had begun thirty-seven days earlier.

Now that the active campaign had ended, both armies got on with the business of preparing for what would come next. Nathan Bedford Forrest and his weary riders moved to Corinth, Mississippi, to rest, remount and refit as best they could. The three Confederate infantry corps moved, by separate routes, to Tupelo, Mississippi, where they would take stock of their losses, consolidate their decimated units and reorganize.

Major General George Thomas's Federal army, instead of consolidating, began to fragment. T.J. Wood's IV Corps, which had led the pursuit, had moved as far south as Lexington, Alabama, when the pursuit ended. It was then sent east and on January 5, 1865, arrived at Huntsville, Alabama, where it built winter quarters and stayed for some time.

Major General A.J. Smith's XVI Corps had followed the IV Corps as far as Pulaski but was then sent west through Lawrenceburg and Waynesboro to Clifton, on the Tennessee River. From there, it was floated down the river to Eastport, Mississippi. By January 19, elements of the corps had patrolled as far west as Corinth.

Major General John M. Schofield's XXIII Corps had moved south as far as Columbia when the pursuit of Hood's army ended. It was then also sent west to the Tennessee River at Clifton, where the men boarded steamers for Cincinnati. They would eventually be sent to North Carolina.

Finally, Major General James B. Steedman's Provisional Division, District of the Etowah, whose USCT troops had suffered so much at Granbury's Lunette and Peach Orchard Hill, was sent to reoccupy Decatur, Alabama, which it managed to do on December 27. Steedman then moved about twenty miles toward Tuscumbia before being ordered to take his command back to Chattanooga on January 1.

Epilogue

As historian James Lee McDonough noted in his excellent book on the Battle of Nashville, the Tennessee Campaign was the Confederacy's last great gamble. In the "Old Army," before the war, John Bell Hood was known as a gambler, and in battle, he had built a reputation as a brave and aggressive commander. In large part because of this reputation, he was given command of the Army of Tennessee at a critical time when such attributes were thought to be the only thing that might save the city of Atlanta. When Hood proposed the Tennessee Campaign in late October, his superiors, P.G.T. Beauregard and Jefferson Davis, agreed, whatever their reservations. But from the time the army marched away from the Tennessee River on November 21, it was Hood's campaign to win or lose. The threat that Hood and his army posed was certainly taken seriously by the Federal high command, and for almost two months, the campaign shared the headlines with Sherman's campaign in Georgia.

The campaign itself was a long-odds gamble from the beginning and involved, as all such campaigns do, a series of critical decisions that, in the end, determined the outcome. For the Army of Tennessee, probably the most critical moment was Hood's decision to continue on to Nashville after the debacle at Franklin. Hood said that his decision was made out of his concern for the morale of the army and based on the hope of reinforcements from Trans-Mississippi and the possibility of a mistake on the part of George Thomas and his army. Betting on help from Texas when the U.S. Navy controlled the Mississippi River and the Gulf coast seems like wishful thinking. Hoping for a colossal blunder on the part of a general who had been his teacher at West Point and was possibly the most professional and competent soldier in the U.S. Army—and whose forces outnumbered his at least two to one—seems like the longest-odds bet of all. In the end, John Bell Hood simply overplayed his hand, and George Thomas made him and the army he led pay a terrible price.

The cost of the campaign is difficult to measure. Accurate numbers are hard to come by, as many historians have discovered. Federal casualties for the three major engagements—Spring Hill, Franklin and Nashville—plus the retreat probably didn't much exceed 6,000. The Confederate casualties are more difficult to calculate. Eric Jacobson, a historian in Middle Tennessee who has made a detailed study of casualties in Hood's army, says that, according to the numbers available, out of about 33,200 troops effective for duty at the beginning of the campaign, Hood seems to have have suffered almost 16,000 casualties. Allowing for wounded men who returned to duty, by mid-January, the army's strength was listed at 20,700. Jacobson sums it up this way: "The losses suffered by the Confederates during the Tennessee Campaign were staggering. Nearly forty per cent of Hood's army had been lost, and the troops that remained were nearing collapse. The invasion to win back Tennessee had ended in abysmal failure."[170]

On December 30, Brigadier General Thomas J. Wood, commanding the IV Corps, wrote to headquarters:

> *I feel confident that Hood has not taken across the Tennessee River more than half the men he brought across it; that no more than half of those taken out were armed; that he lost three fourths of his artillery and, that for rout, demoralization, even disintegration, the condition of his command is without parallel in this war.*[171]

General Wood's official reports often show a marked tendency toward embellishment and hyperbole, but in this case, he might not be far wrong.

By January 1865, the Confederate States of America was on its last legs—it had just over three months to live. On January 23, John Bell Hood was relieved, at his own request, as the army's commander. What remained of the Army of Tennessee was reorganized and sent to the east to fight Sherman. It surrendered with Joseph E. Johnston in North Carolina on April 26, 1865.

On his last day in command, Hood issued the following statement to the men who had followed him through Tennessee:

HEADQUARTERS ARMY OF TENNESSEE, Tupelo, Miss., January 23, 1865.

SOLDIERS: At my request I have this day been relieved from the command of this army. In taking leave of you accept my thanks for the patience with which you have endured your many hardships during the recent campaign. I am alone responsible for its conception, and strived hard to do my duty in its execution. I urge upon you the importance of giving your entire support to the distinguished soldier who now assumes command, and I shall look with deep interest upon all your future operations and rejoice at your successes.

J.B. HOOD, General.

John Bell Hood is one of the most controversial, interesting and ultimately tragic characters to come out of the Civil War, and the campaign he led into Tennessee stands as one of the greatest disasters suffered by any army during that great conflict. A great many people have voiced their opinions and evaluations of Hood and his career, but a Tennessee farmer, writing seventeen years after the war, offered an assessment that has stood the test of time. Private Samuel Rush "Sam" Watkins, Company H, First Tennessee Infantry, was in the Army of Tennessee from its beginning and served under Hood during the Atlanta and Tennessee Campaigns. In his memoirs, published in 1882, he wrote, "Hood was a good man, a kind man, a philanthropic man…As a soldier, he was brave, noble, and gallant, and fought with the ferociousness of a wounded tiger and with the everlasting grip of a bull dog; but, as a General he was a failure in every particular."

Through the bitter disappointment of the missed opportunity at Spring Hill, the appalling bloodbath at Franklin, the crushing defeat at Nashville and the brutal, freezing retreat to the Tennessee River, John Bell Hood led the Army of Tennessee in the Confederacy's last high-stakes gamble—and lost. In the end, John Bell Hood's military career was over, George Henry Thomas's reputation as the consummate professional soldier was vindicated and the Confederacy's last real hope on the battlefield was gone.

The Commanders

General John Bell Hood

Hood survived the war and moved to New Orleans, where he became a cotton broker and an insurance executive. In 1868, he married Anna Marie Hennen, with whom he fathered eleven children over a span of ten years, including three sets of twins. In 1879, a yellow fever epidemic destroyed Hood's insurance business and then killed him, his wife and his eldest child. Hood's ten destitute orphans were placed in good homes through the efforts of his friends from the army. Hood spent several years writing his memoirs, *Advance and Retreat: Personal Experiences in the United States and Confederate Armies*, in which he devoted a good deal of space to defending his decisions and his conduct of the Tennessee Campaign. The book was published the year after his death through the efforts of General P.G.T. Beauregard.

Major General George Henry Thomas

After the Battle of Nashville and the pursuit of Hood's army, Thomas received the thanks of the president and Congress and was made a major general in the regular army. Thomas supposedly remarked to an aide that he had already earned the promotion a year earlier at Chattanooga. He never quite forgave Grant and the War Department in Washington for their harassment during the Tennessee Campaign. Thomas never really got over what he considered unfair and unwarranted treatment by Grant, Sherman and the people in Washington during the lead-up to the Battle of Nashville. The twenty-five-year veteran once said to a subordinate: "They treat me as if I were a boy, and incapable of planning a campaign or fighting a battle. If they will let me alone I will fight the battle…and will surely win it."[172]

During the war, Thomas destroyed two Confederate armies and saved at least one Federal one at Chickamauga. After the war, Thomas was given command of the Division of the Pacific. He died of a stroke at his headquarters at the Presidio in San Francisco on March 28, 1870, at the age of fifty-three. He never wrote his memoirs, having destroyed his personal papers rather than see "his life hawked in print for the eyes of the curious." He was buried in his wife's hometown of Troy, New York. Since he stayed with the Union, none of his family from Virginia came to the funeral.

Franklin Order of Battle

Key for individuals:

killed: (k)
mortally wounded: (mw)
wounded: (w)
captured: (c)

Key for units, where available:

killed: K
wounded: W
missing: M

ARMY OF THE OHIO
Major General John M. Schofield

IV CORPS
Major General David S. Stanley (w)

DIVISION	BRIGADE	REGIMENTS AND OTHERS
1st Division Brigadier General Nathan Kimball	1st Brigade Colonel Isaac M. Kirby (K-2, W-8, M-4 =14)	21st Illinois—Captain William H. Jamison 38th Illinois—Captain Andrew M. Pollard 31st Indiana—Colonel John T. Smith 81st Indiana—Major Edward G. Mathey 90th Ohio—Lieutenant Colonel Samuel N. Yeoman 101st Ohio—Lieutenant Colonel Bedan B. McDanald
	2nd Brigade Brigadier General Walter C. Whitaker (K-0, W-5, M-4 =9)	96th Illinois—Major George Hicks 115th Illinois—Colonel Jesse H. Moore 35th Indiana—Lieutenant Colonel Augustus G. Tassin 21st Kentucky—Lieutenant Colonel James C. Evans 23rd Kentucky—Lieutenant Colonel George W. Northup 40th Ohio (six companies)—Lieutenant Colonel James Watson 45th Ohio—Lieutenant Colonel John H. Humphrey 51st Ohio—Lieutenant Colonel Charles H. Wood
	3rd Brigade Brigadier General William Grose (K-3, W-24, M-10 =37)	75th Illinois—Colonel John E. Bennett 80th Illinois—Captain James Cunningham 84th Illinois—Lieutenant Colonel Charles H. Morton 9th Indiana—Colonel Isaac C.B. Suman 30th Indiana (three companies)—Captain Henry W. Lawton 36th Indiana (one company)—Lieutenant John P. Swisher 84th Indiana—Major John C. Taylor 77th Pennsylvania—Colonel Thomas E. Rose

DIVISION	BRIGADE	REGIMENTS AND OTHERS
2nd Division Brigadier General George D. Wagner	1st Brigade Colonel Emerson Opdycke (K-16, W-125, M-65 =206)	36th Illinois—Major Levi P. Holden 44th Illinois—Lieutenant Colonel John Russell 73rd Illinois—Major Thomas W. Motherspaw 74th/88th Illinois—Lieutenant Colonel George W. Smith 125th Ohio—Captain Edward P. Bates 24th Wisconsin—Major Arthur MacArthur
	2nd Brigade Colonel John Q. Lane (K-29, W-269, M-340 =638)	100th Illinois—Lieutenant Colonel Charles M. Hammond 40th Indiana—Lieutenant Colonel Henry Leaming 57th Indiana—Major John S. McGraw 28th Kentucky—Lieutenant J. Rowan Boone 26th Ohio—Captain William Clark 97th Ohio—Lieutenant Colonel Milton Barnes
	3rd Brigade Colonel Joseph Conrad (K-7, W-125, M-265 =397)	42nd Illinois—Major Frederick A. Atwater 51st Illinois—Captain Merritt B. Atwater 79th Illinois—Colonel Allen Buckner 15th Missouri—Captain George Ernst 64th Ohio—Lieutenant Colonel Robert C. Brown 65th Ohio Major Orlow Smith

DIVISION	BRIGADE	REGIMENTS AND OTHERS
3rd Division Brigadier General Thomas J. Wood	1st Brigade Colonel Abel D. Streight	89th Illinois—Lieutenant Colonel William D. Williams 51st Indiana—Captain William W. Scearce 8th Kansas—Lieutenant Colonel John Conover 15th Ohio—Colonel Frank Askew 49th Ohio—Major Luther M. Strong
	2nd Brigade Colonel Philip S. Post	59th Illinois—Major James M. Stookey 41st Ohio—Lieutenant Colonel Robert L. Kimberly 71st Ohio—Colonel Henry K. McConnell 93rd Ohio—Lieutenant Colonel Daniel Bowman 124th Ohio—Lieutenant Colonel James Pickands
	3rd Brigade Colonel Frederick Knefler	79th Indiana—Lieutenant Colonel George W. Parker 86th Indiana—Colonel George F. Dick 13th Ohio (battalion)—Major Joseph T. Snider 19th Ohio—Lieutenant Colonel Henry G. Stratton 17th Kentucky—Colonel A.M. Stout
	Artillery Captain Lyman Bridges	Bridges's Illinois Battery—Lieutenant Lyman A. White 1st Kentucky Battery—Captain Theodore S. Thomasson Battery A, 1st Ohio Light—Lieutenant Charles W. Scovill Battery G, 1st Ohio Light—Captain Alexander Marshall 6th Ohio Battery—Lieutenant Aaron P. Baldwin 20th Ohio Battery—Lieutenant John S. Burdick Battery B, Pennsylvania Light—Captain Jacob Ziegler Battery M, 4th U.S. Light—Lieutenant Samuel Canby

XXIII CORPS
Brigadier General Jacob D. Cox

DIVISION	BRIGADE	REGIMENTS AND OTHERS
2nd Division Brigadier General Thomas H. Ruger	2nd Brigade Colonel Orlando H. Moore (K-21, W-89, M-12 = 122)	107th Illinois—Lieutenant Colonel Francis H. Lowry 80th Indiana—Lieutenant Colonel Alfred D. Owen 129th Indiana—Colonel Charles A. Zollinger 23rd Michigan—Colonel Oliver L. Spaulding 111th Ohio—Lieutenant Colonel Isaac R. Sherwood 118th Ohio—Major Edgar Sowers
	3rd Brigade Colonel Silas Strickland (K-73, W-178, M-280 = 531)	72nd Illinois—Lieutenant Colonel Joseph Stockton 44th Missouri—Colonel Robert C. Bradshaw 50th Ohio—Lieutenant Colonel Hamilton S. Gillespie 183rd Ohio—Colonel George W. Hoge

DIVISION	BRIGADE	REGIMENTS AND OTHERS
3rd Division Brigadier General James W. Reilly	1st Brigade Brigadier General James W. Reilly (K-33, W-130, M-70 = 233)	12th Kentucky—Lieutenant Colonel Laurence H. Rousseau 16th Kentucky—Lieutenant Colonel John S. White 100th Ohio—Lieutenant Colonel Edwin L. Hayes 104th Ohio—Colonel Oscar W. Sterl 175th Ohio—Lieutenant Colonel Daniel W. McCoy 8th Tennessee—Captain James W. Berry
	2nd Brigade Colonel John S. Casement (K-3, W-16, M-0 = 19)	65th Illinois—Lieutenant Colonel W. Scott Stewart 65th Indiana—Lieutenant Colonel John W. Hammond 124th Indiana—Colonel John M. Orr 103rd Ohio—Captain Henry S. Pickands 5th Tennessee—Major David G. Bowers
	3rd Brigade Colonel Israel N. Stiles (K-11, W-51, M-21 = 83)	112th Illinois—Lieutenant Colonel Emery S. Bond 63rd Indiana—Lieutenant Colonel Daniel Morris 120th Indiana—Colonel Allen W. Prather 128th Indiana—Lieutenant Colonel Jasper Packard

CAVALRY CORPS

Major General James H. Wilson
Escort: 4th U.S. Cavalry, Lieutenant Joseph Hedges

DIVISION	BRIGADE	REGIMENTS AND OTHERS
1st Division Brigadier General Edward M. McCook	1st Brigade Brigadier General John T. Croxton	8th Iowa Cavalry Colonel Joseph B. Dorr 4th Kentucky Mounted Infantry—Colonel Robert M. Kelly 2nd Michigan Cavalry—Colonel Benjamin Smith 1st Tennessee Cavalry—Lieutenant Colonel Calvin M. Dyer
5th Division Brigadier General Edward Hatch	1st Brigade Colonel Robert R. Stewart	3rd Illinois Cavalry—Lieutenant Colonel Robert H. Carnahan 11th Indiana Cavalry—Lieutenant Colonel Abram Sharra
	2nd Brigade Colonel Datus E. Coon	2nd Iowa Cavalry—Major Charles C. Horton 6th Illinois Cavalry—Lieutenant Colonel John Lynch 7th Illinois Cavalry—Major John M. Graham 9th Illinois Cavalry—Captain Joseph W. Harper 12th Tennessee Cavalry—Colonel George Spalding
6th Division Brigadier General Richard W. Johnson	1st Brigade Colonel Thomas J. Harrison	16th Illinois Cavalry—Major Charles H. Beeres 5th Iowa Cavalry—Major J. Morris Young 7th Ohio Cavalry—Colonel Israel Garrard
	2nd Brigade Colonel James Biddle	14th Illinois Cavalry—Major Francis M. Davidson 6th Indiana Cavalry—Major Jacob S. Stephens 8th Michigan Cavalry—Lieutenant Colonel Grover S. Wormer 3rd Tennessee—Major Benjamin Cunningham

ARMY OF TENNESSEE
General John B. Hood, Commanding

LEE'S CORPS
Lieutenant General Stephen D. Lee

DIVISION	BRIGADE	REGIMENTS AND OTHERS
Johnson's Division Major General Edward Johnson	Deas's Brigade Brigadier General Zachariah C. Deas (w)	19th Alabama 22nd Alabama 25th Alabama 39th Alabama 50th Alabama
	Manigault's Brigade Brigadier General Arthur M. Manigault (w) Lieutenant Colonel William L. Butler	24th Alabama 28th Alabama 34th Alabama 10th South Carolina 19th South Carolina
	Sharp's Brigade Brigadier General Jacob H. Sharp	7th Mississippi 9th Mississippi 10th Mississippi 41st Mississippi 44th Mississippi 9th Mississippi Sharpshooters Battalion
	Brantley's Brigade Brigadier General William F. Brantley	24th and 27th Mississippi 29th and 30th Mississippi 34th Mississippi Dismounted Cavalry Company

DIVISION	BRIGADE	REGIMENTS AND OTHERS
Stevenson's Division Major General Carter L. Stevenson	Cummings's Brigade Colonel Elihu P. Watkins	24th Georgia 36th Georgia 39th Georgia 56th Georgia
	Pettus's Brigade Brigadier General Edmund W. Pettus	20th Alabama 23rd Alabama 30th Alabama 31st Alabama 46th Alabama
	Brown's and Reynolds's Brigades Colonel Joseph B. Palmer	60th North Carolina—Major James T. Huff 3rd and 18th Tennessee—Lieutenant Colonel William R. Butler 23rd, 26th and 45th Tennessee—Colonel Anderson Searcy 32nd Tennessee—Colonel John P. McGuire 54th Virginia Infantry—Captain William G. Anderson 63rd Virginia Infantry—Lieutenant Connally H. Lynch

DIVISION	BRIGADE	REGIMENTS AND OTHERS
Clayton's Division Major General Henry D. Clayton Sr.	Stovall's Brigade Brigadier General Marcellus A. Stovall	40th Georgia 41st Georgia 42nd Georgia 43rd Georgia 52nd Georgia
	Gibson's Brigade Brigadier General Randall L. Gibson	1st Louisiana 4th Louisiana 13th and 20th Louisiana 16th and 25th Louisiana 19th Louisiana 30th Louisiana 4th Louisiana Battalion 14th Louisiana Sharpshooters Battalion
	Holtzclaw's Brigade Brigadier General James Holtzclaw	18th Alabama 32nd Alabama 36th Alabama 38th Alabama 58th Alabama
Corps Artillery Colonel Robert F. Beckham (mw) Major John W. Johnston	Courtney's Battalion Captain James P. Douglas	Dent's Alabama Battery Douglas's Texas Battery Garrity's Alabama Battery
	Eldridge's Battalion Captain Charles E. Fenner	Eufaula, Alabama Battery Fenner's Louisiana Battery Stanford's Miss Battery
	Johnson's Battalion Captain John B. Rowan	Corput's Georgia Battery Marshall's Tenn Battery Stephens's Light Artillery

Stewart's Corps
Lieutenant General Alexander P. Stewart

Division	Brigade	Regiments and Others
Loring's Division Major General William W. Loring	Featherston's Brigade Brigadier General Winfield S. Featherston	1st Mississippi 3rd Mississippi 22nd Mississippi 31st Mississippi 33rd Mississippi 40th Mississippi 1st Mississippi Battalion
	Adams's Brigade Brigadier General John Adams (k) Colonel Robert Lowry	6th Mississippi 14th Mississippi 15th Mississippi 20th Mississippi 23rd Mississippi 43rd Mississippi
	Scott's Brigade Brigadier General Thomas M. Scott (w) Colonel John Snodgrass	27th Alabama 35th Alabama 49th Alabama 55th Alabama 57th Alabama 12th Louisiana

DIVISION	BRIGADE	REGIMENTS AND OTHERS
French's Division Major General Samuel G. French	Ector's Brigade Colonel David Coleman (not present at Franklin)	29th North Carolina 30th North Carolina 9th Texas 10th Texas Cavalry (dismounted) 14th Texas Cavalry (dismounted) 32nd Texas Cavalry (dismounted)
	Cockrell's Brigade Brigadier General Francis M. Cockrell (w) Colonel Peter C. Flournoy	1st Missouri 2nd Missouri 3rd Missouri 4th Missouri 5th Missouri 6th Missouri 1st Missouri Cavalry (dismounted) 3rd Missouri Cavalry Battalion (dismounted)
	Sears's Brigade Brigadier General Claudius Sears	4th Mississippi 35th Mississippi 36th Mississippi 39th Mississippi 46th Mississippi 7th Mississippi Battalion

DIVISION	BRIGADE	REGIMENTS AND OTHERS
Walthall's Division Major General Edward C. Walthall	Quarles's Brigade Brigadier General William A. Quarles (wounded at Franklin, captured December 17) Brigadier General George D. Johnston (Nashville)	1st Alabama 42nd Tennessee 46th Tennessee 48th Tennessee 49th Tennessee 53rd Tennessee 55th Tennessee
	Cantey's Brigade Brigadier General Charles M. Shelley	17th Alabama 26th Alabama 29th Alabama 37th Mississippi
	Reynolds's Brigade Brigadier General Daniel H. Reynolds	4th Arkansas 9th Arkansas 25th Arkansas 1st Arkansas Mounted Rifles (dismounted) 2nd Arkansas Mounted Rifles (dismounted)
Corps Artillery Lieutenant Samuel C. Williams	Truehart's Battalion	Lumsden's Alabama Battery Selden's Alabama Battery
	Myrick's Battalion	Bouanchaud's Louisiana Battery Cowan's Miss Battery Darden's Miss Battery
	Storrs's Battalion	Guibor's Missouri Battery Hoskin's Miss Battery Kolb's Alabama Battery

CHEATHAM'S CORPS
Major General Benjamin F. Cheatham

DIVISION	BRIGADE	REGIMENTS AND OTHERS
Cleburne's Division Major General Patrick Cleburne (k) Brigadier General James A. Smith	Lowrey's Brigade Brigadier General Mark P. Lowrey	16th Alabama 33rd Alabama 45th Alabama 5th Mississippi 8th Mississippi 32nd Mississippi 3rd Mississippi Battalion
	Govan's Brigade Brigadier General Daniel C. Govan	1st and 15th Arkansas 2nd and 24th Arkansas 5th and 13th Arkansas 6th and 7th Arkansas 8th and 19th Arkansas 3rd Confederate
	Granbury's Brigade Brigadier General Hiram B. Granbury (k) Captain E.T. Broughton	5th Confederate 35th Tennessee 6th and 10th Texas 7th Texas 15th Texas 17th, 18th, 24th and 25th Texas Cavalry (dismounted) Nutt's Louisiana Cavalry (dismounted)
	Smith's Brigade (on detached duty) Brigadier General James A. Smith Colonel Charles H. Olmstead	54th Georgia 57th Georgia 63rd Georgia 1st Georgia Volunteers

DIVISION	BRIGADE	REGIMENTS AND OTHERS
Brown's (Cheatham's old) Division Major General John C. Brown (w) Brigadier General Mark P. Lowrey	Gist's Brigade Brigadier General States Rights Gist (k) Lieutenant Colonel Zachariah L. Watters	46th Georgia 65th Georgia 2nd Georgia Sharpshooters Battalion 16th South Carolina 24th South Carolina
	Maney's Brigade Brigadier General John C. Carter (mw) Colonel Hume R. Field	1st and 27th Tennessee 4th Tennessee (provisional) 6th and 9th Tennessee 8th Tennessee 16th Tennessee 28th Tennessee 50th Tennessee
	Strahl's Brigade Brigadier General Otho F. Strahl (k) Colonel Andrew J. Kellar	4th and 5th Tennessee 19th Tennessee 24th Tennessee 31st Tennessee 33rd Tennessee 38th Tennessee 41st Tennessee
	Vaughan's Brigade Brigadier General George W. Gordon (c) Colonel William M. Watkins	11th Tennessee 12th and 47th Tennessee 13th and 154th Tennessee 29th Tennessee 51st and 52nd Tennessee

DIVISION	BRIGADE	REGIMENTS AND OTHERS
Bate's Division Major General William B. Bate	Tyler's Brigade Brigadier General Thomas B. Smith	37th Georgia 4th Georgia Sharpshooters Battalion 2nd Tennessee 10th Tennessee 20th Tennessee 37th Tennessee
	Finley's Brigade Colonel Robert Bullock Major Jacob A. Lash	1st and 3rd Florida 4th Florida 6th Florida 7th Florida 1st Florida Cavalry (dismounted)
	Jackson's Brigade Brigadier General Henry R. Jackson	25th Georgia 29th Georgia 30th Georgia 1st Georgia Confederate 1st Georgia Sharpshooters Battalion
Corps Artillery Colonel Melancthon Smith	Hoxton's Battalion	Phelan's Alabama Battery Perry's Florida Battery Turner's Miss Battery
	Hotchkiss's Battalion	Goldthwaite's Alabama Battery Key's Arkansas Battery Bledsoe's Missouri Battery
	Cobb's Battalion	Slocumb's Louisiana Battery Ferguson's South Carolina Battery Phillip's (Mabane's) Tennessee Battery

CAVALRY CORPS
Major General Nathan B. Forrest

DIVISION	BRIGADE	REGIMENTS AND OTHERS
Chalmers's Division Brigadier General James R. Chalmers	Rucker's Brigade Colonel Edmund W. Rucker	7th Alabama Cavalry 5th Mississippi Cavalry 7th Tennessee Cavalry 12th Tennessee Cavalry 14th Tennessee Cavalry 15th Tennessee Cavalry Forrest's Regiment, Tennessee Cavalry
	Biffle's Brigade Colonel Jacob B. Biffle	4th Tennessee Cavalry 9th Tennessee Cavalry 10th Tennessee Cavalry
Buford's Division Brigadier General Abraham Buford	Bell's Brigade Colonel Tyree H. Bell	2nd/22nd Tennessee Cavalry (Barteau's) 19th Tennessee Cavalry 20th Tennessee Cavalry 21st Tennessee Cavalry Nixon's Tennessee Cavalry Regiment
	Crossland's Brigade Colonel Edward Crossland	3rd Kentucky Mounted Infantry 7th Kentucky Mounted Infantry 8th Kentucky Mounted Infantry 12th Kentucky Cavalry Huey's Kentucky Battalion
Jackson's Division Brigadier General William H. Jackson	Armstrong's Brigade Brigadier General Frank C. Armstrong	1st Mississippi Cavalry 2nd Mississippi Cavalry 28th Mississippi Cavalry Ballentine's Mississippi Regiment
	Ross's Brigade Brigadier General Lawrence S. Ross	3rd Texas Cavalry 6th Texas Cavalry 9th Texas Cavalry 27th Texas Cavalry 1st Texas Legion
Artillery	Morton's Tennessee Battery	

Nashville Order of Battle

ARMY OF THE CUMBERLAND
Major General George H. Thomas, commanding

HEADQUARTERS
Chief of Staff: Brigadier General William D. Whipple

IV CORPS
Brigadier General Thomas J. Wood

DIVISION	BRIGADE	REGIMENTS AND OTHERS
1st Division Brigadier General Nathan Kimball	1st Brigade Colonel Isaac M. Kirby	21st Illinois—Captain William H. Jamison 38th Illinois—Captain Andrew M. Pollard 31st Indiana—Colonel John T. Smith 81st Indiana—Major Edward G. Mathey 90th Ohio—Lieutenant Colonel Samuel N. Yeoman 101st Ohio—Lieutenant Colonel Bedan B. McDonald
	2nd Brigade Brigadier General Walter C. Whitaker	96th Illinois—Major George Hicks 115th Illinois—Colonel Jesse H. Moore 35th Indiana—Lieutenant Colonel Augustus G. Tassin 21st Kentucky—Lieutenant Colonel James C. Evans 23rd Kentucky—Lieutenant Colonel George W. Northup 45th Ohio—Lieutenant Colonel John H. Humphrey 51st Ohio—Lieutenant Colonel Charles H. Wood
	3rd Brigade Brigadier General William Grose	75th Illinois—Colonel John E. Bennett 80th Illinois—Captain James Cunningham 84th Illinois—Lieutenant Colonel Charles H. Morton 9th Indiana—Colonel Isaac C.B. Suman 30th Indiana—Captain Henry W. Lawton 36th Indiana (one company)—Lieutenant John P. Swisher 84th Indiana—Major John C. Taylor 77th Pennsylvania—Colonel Thomas E. Rose

Division	Brigade	Regiments and Others
2nd Division Brigadier General Washington Lafayette Elliott	1st Brigade Colonel Emerson Opdycke	36th Illinois—Major Levi P. Holden 44th Illinois—Captain Alonzo W. Clark 74th Illinois—Captain Wilson Burroughs 74th and 88th Illinois—Lieutenant Colonel George W. Smith 125th Ohio—Major Joseph Bruff 24th Wisconsin—Captain William Kennedy
	2nd Brigade Colonel John Q. Lane	100th Illinois—Lieutenant Colonel Charles M. Hammend 40th Indiana—Lieutenant Colonel Henry Leaming 57th Indiana—Lieutenant Colonel Willis Blanch (w), Major John S. McGraw 28th Kentucky—Major George W. Barth, Lieutenant Colonel J. Rowan Boone 26th Ohio—Captain William Clark 97th Ohio—Lieutenant Colonel Milton Barnes (w), Captain Clarkson C. Nichols
	3rd Brigade Colonel Joseph Conrad	42nd Illinois—Lieutenant Colonel Edgar D. Swain 51st Illinois—Captain Albert M. Tilton 79th Illinois—Colonel Allen Buckner 15th Missouri—Captain George Ernst 64th Ohio—Lieutenant Colonel Robert Carson Brown 65th Ohio—Major Orlow Smith

DIVISION	BRIGADE	REGIMENTS AND OTHERS
Third Division Brigadier General Samuel Beatty	1st Brigade Colonel Abel D. Streight	89th Illinois—Lieutenant Colonel William D. Williams 51st Indiana—Captain William W. Scearce 8th Kansas—Lieutenant Colonel John Conover 15th Ohio—Colonel Frank Askew (w), Lieutenant Colonel John McClenahan 49th Ohio—Major Luther M. Strong (w), Captain Daniel Hartsough
	2nd Brigade Colonel Philip S. Post (w) Lieutenant Colonel Robert L. Kimberly	59th Illinois—Major James M. Stookey 41st Ohio—Lieutenant Colonel Robert L. Kimberly, Captain Ezra Dunham 71st Ohio—Lieutenant Colonel James H. Hart (w), Captain William H. McClure 93rd Ohio—Lieutenant Colonel Daniel Bowman 124th Ohio—Lieutenant Colonel James Pickands
	3rd Brigade Colonel Frederick Knefler	79th Indiana—Lieutenant Colonel George W. Parker 86th Indiana—Colonel George F. Dick 13th Ohio (four companies)—Major Joseph T. Snider 19th Ohio—Lieutenant Colonel Henry G. Stratton

XXIII CORPS
Major General John M. Schofield

DIVISION	BRIGADE	REGIMENTS AND OTHERS
2nd Division Major General Darius N. Couch	1st Brigade Brigadier General Joseph A. Cooper	130th Indiana—Colonel Charles S. Parrish 26th Kentucky—Colonel Cicero Maxwell 25th Michigan—Captain Samuel L. Demarest 99th Ohio—Lieutenant Colonel John E. Cummins 3rd Tennessee—Colonel William Cross 6th Tennessee—Lieutenant Colonel Edward Maynard
	2nd Brigade Colonel Orlando H. Moore	107th Illinois—Captain John W. Wood 80th Indiana—Lieutenant Colonel Alfred D. Owen 129th Indiana—Colonel Charles A. Zollinger 23rd Michigan—Colonel Oliver L. Spaulding 111th Ohio—Lieutenant Colonel Isaac R. Sherwood 118th Ohio—Major Edgar Sowers
	3rd Brigade Colonel John Mehringer	91st Indiana—Lieutenant Colonel Charles H. Butterfield 123rd Indiana—Colonel John C. McQuiston 50th Ohio—Lieutenant Colonel Hamilton S. Gillespie 183rd Ohio—Colonel George W. Hoge

DIVISION	BRIGADE	REGIMENTS AND OTHERS
3rd Division Brigadier General Jacob D. Cox	1st Brigade Colonel Charles C. Doolittle	12th Kentucky—Lieutenant Colonel Laurence H. Rousseau 16th Kentucky—Captain Jacob Miller 100th Ohio—Lieutenant Colonel Edwin L. Hayes 104th Ohio—Colonel Oscar W. Sterl 8th Tennessee—Captain James W. Berry
	2nd Brigade Colonel John S. Casement	65th Illinois—Lieutenant Colonel W. Scott Stewart 65th Indiana—Lieutenant Colonel John W. Hammond 124th Indiana—Colonel John M. Orr 103rd Ohio—Captain Henry S. Pickands 5th Tennessee—Lieutenant Colonel Nathaniel Witt
	3rd Brigade Colonel Israel N. Stiles	112th Illinois—Major Tristram T. Dow 63rd Indiana—Lieutenant Colonel Daniel Morris 120th Indiana—Major John M. Barcus 128th Indiana—Lieutenant Colonel Jasper Packard
Artillery		15th Battery, Indiana Light—Captain Alonzo D. Harvey 19th Battery, Ohio Light—Captain Frank Wilson 23rd Battery, Indiana Light—Lieutenant Aaron A. Wilber Battery D, 1st Ohio Light—Captain Giles J. Cockerill

DETACHMENT, ARMY OF THE TENNESSEE
Major General Andrew J. Smith

DIVISION	BRIGADE	REGIMENTS AND OTHERS
1st Division Brigadier General John McArthur	1st Brigade Colonel William L. McMillen	114th Illinois—Captain John M. Johnson 93rd Indiana—Colonel DeWitt C. Thomas, Captain Charles A. Hubbard 10th Minnesota—Lieutenant Colonel Samuel P. Jennison (w), Captain Edwin C. Sanders 72nd Ohio—Lieutenant Colonel Charles G. Eaton 95th Ohio—Lieutenant Colonel Jefferson Brumback Cogswell's Battery, Illinois Light Artillery—Lieutenant S. Hamilton McClaury
	2nd Brigade Colonel Lucius F. Hubbard	5th Minnesota—Lieutenant Colonel William B. Gere 9th Minnesota—Colonel Josiah F. Marsh 11th Missouri—Lieutenant Colonel Eli Bowyer (w), Major Modesta J. Green 8th Wisconsin—Lieutenant Colonel William B. Britton 2nd Battery, Iowa Light Artillery—Captain Joseph R. Reed
	3rd Brigade Colonel Sylvester G. Hill (k) Colonel William R. Marshall	12th Iowa—Lieutenant Colonel John H. Stibbs 35th Iowa—Major William Dill, Captain Abraham N. Snyder 7th Minnesota—Colonel William R. Marshall, Lieutenant George Bradley 33rd Missouri—Lieutenant Colonel William H. Heath Battery I, 2nd Missouri Light Artillery—Captain Stephen H. Julian

DIVISION	BRIGADE	REGIMENTS AND OTHERS
2nd Division Brigadier General Kenner Garrard	1st Brigade Colonel David Moore	119th Illinois—Colonel Thomas J. Kinney 122nd Illinois—Lieutenant Colonel James F. Drish 89th Indiana—Lieutenant Colonel Hervey Craven 21st Missouri—Lieutenant Colonel Edwin Moore 9th Battery, Indiana Light Artillery—Lieutenant Samuel G. Calfee
	2nd Brigade Colonel James I. Gilbert	58th Illinois—Major Robert W. Healy 27th Iowa—Lieutenant Colonel Jed Lake 32nd Iowa— Lieutenant Colonel Gustavus A. Eberhart 10th Kansas (four companies)—Captain William C. Jones 3rd Battery, Indiana Light Artillery—Lieutenant Thomas J. Ginn
	3rd Brigade Colonel Edward H. Wolfe	49th Illinois—Colonel Phineas Pease 117th Illinois— Lieutenant Colonel Jonathan Merriam 52nd Indiana— Lieutenant Colonel Zalmon S. Main 178th New York—Captain John B. Gandolfo Battery G, 2nd Illinois Light Artillery—Captain John W. Lowell

Nashville Order of Battle

Division	Brigade	Regiments and Others
3rd Division Colonel Jonathan B. Moore	1st Brigade Colonel Lyman M. Ward	72nd Illinois—Captain James A. Sexton 40th Missouri—Colonel Samuel A. Holmes 14th Wisconsin—Major Eddy F. Ferris 33rd Wisconsin—Lieutenant Colonel Frederick S. Lovell
	2nd Brigade Colonel Leander Blanden	81st Illinois— Lieutenant Colonel Andrew W. Rogers 95th Illinois— Lieutenant Colonel William Avery 44th Missouri— Lieutenant Colonel Andrew J. Barr
Artillery		14th Battery, Indiana Light—Captain Francis W. Morse Battery A, 2nd Missouri Light—Lieutenant John Zepp

PROVISIONAL DETACHMENT (DISTRICT OF THE ETOWAH)
Major General James B. Steedman

DIVISION	BRIGADE	REGIMENTS AND OTHERS
Provisional Division Brigadier General Charles Cruft	1st Brigade Col Benjamin Harrison	Three battalions detached from the XX Corps
	2nd Brigade [Army of the Tennessee] Colonel John G. Mitchell	Consisted of men on detached duty from the Army of the Tennessee
	3rd Brigade Lieutenant Colonel Charles H. Grosvenor	68th Indiana— Lieutenant Colonel Harvey J. Espy 18th Ohio—Captain Ebenezer Grosvenor (k), Captain John M. Benedict (w), Lieutenant Charles Grant 2nd Battalion, XIV Army Corps—Captain D.H. Henderson (w)
	Artillery	20th Battery, Indiana Light—Captain Milton A. Osborne 18th Ohio Battery—Captain Charles C. Aleshire
U.S. Colored Troops	1st Colored Brigade Colonel Thomas J. Morgan	14th U.S. Colored Troops— Lieutenant Colonel Henry C. Corbin 16th U.S. Colored Troops—Colonel William B. Gaw 17th U.S. Colored Troops—Colonel William R. Shafter 18th U.S. Colored Troops (battalion)—Major Lewis D. Joy 44th U.S. Colored Troops—Colonel Lewis Johnson
	2nd Colored Brigade Colonel Charles R. Thompson	12th U S. Colored Troops— Lieutenant Colonel William R. Sellon, Captain Henry Hegner 13th U.S. Colored Troops—Colonel John A. Hottenstein 100th U.S. Colored Troops—Major Collin Ford 1st Battery, Kansas Light Artillery—Captain Marcus D. Tenney

Division	Brigade	Regiments and Others
Post of Nashville Brigadier General John F. Miller	2nd Brigade, 4th Division, XX Corps Colonel Edwin C. Mason	142nd Indiana— Lieutenant Colonel John M. Comparet 45th New York— Lieutenant Colonel Adolphus Dobke 176th Ohio— Lieutenant Colonel William B. Nesbitt 179th Ohio—Colonel Harley H. Sage 182nd Ohio—Colonel Lewis Butler
	Unattached	3rd Kentucky (part) 28th Michigan—Colonel William W. Wheeler 173rd Ohio—Colonel John R. Hurd 78th Pennsylvania (detachment)—Major Henry W. Torbett Veteran Reserve Corps—Colonel Frank P. Cahill 44th Wisconsin (battalion)—Lieutenant Colonel Oliver C. Bissell 45th Wisconsin (battalion)
	Garrison Artillery Major John J. Ely	Bridges's Battery, Illinois Light—Lieutenant Lyman A. White 2nd Battery, Indiana Light—Captain James S. Whicher 4th Battery, Indiana Light—Captain Benjamin F. Johnson 12th Battery, Indiana Light—Captain James E. White 21st Battery, Indiana Light—Captain Abram Piatt Andrew 22nd Battery, Indiana Light—Captain Edward W. Nicholson 24th Battery, Indiana Light—Lieutenant Hiram Allen

DIVISION	BRIGADE	REGIMENTS AND OTHERS
	Garrison Artillery Major John J. Ely (continued)	Battery F, 1st Michigan Light—Captain Byron D. Paddock
		Battery A, 1st Ohio Light—Lieutenant Charles W. Scovill
		Battery E, 1st Ohio Light—Lieutenant Frank B. Reckard
		20th Battery, Ohio Light—Captain William Backus
		Battery C, 1st Tennessee Light—Lieutenant Joseph Grigsby
		Battery D, 1st Tennessee Light—Captain Samuel D. Leinart
		Battery A, 3rd U.S. Colored Light—Captain Josiah V. Meigs
	Quartermaster's Division Brigadier General James L. Donaldson	Composed of quartermaster's employees

CAVALRY CORPS
Major General James H. Wilson
Escort: 4th United States, Lieutenant Joseph Hedges

DIVISION	BRIGADE	REGIMENTS AND OTHERS
1st Division	1st Brigade Brigadier General John T. Croxton	8th Iowa—Colonel Joseph B. Dorr 4th Kentucky Mounted Infantry—Colonel Robert M. Kelly 2nd Michigan—Lieutenant Colonel Benjamin Smith 1st Tennessee—Lieutenant Colonel Calvin M. Dyer Board of Trade Battery, Illinois Light Artillery—Captain George I. Robinson
	2nd and 3rd Brigades under Brigadier General E.M. McCook in western Kentucky	
5th Division Brigadier General Edward Hatch	1st Brigade Colonel Robert R. Stewart	3rd Illinois—Lieutenant Colonel Robert H. Carnahan 11th Indiana—Lieutenant Colonel Abram Sharra 12th Missouri—Colonel Oliver Wells 10th Tennessee—Major William P. Story (mw), Major James T. Abernathy
	2nd Brigade Colonel Datus E. Coon	6th Illinois—Lieutenant Colonel John Lynch 7th Illinois—Major John M. Graham 9th Illinois—Captain Joseph W. Harper 2nd Iowa—Major Charles C. Horton 12th Tennessee Cavalry—Colonel George Spalding (w) Battery I, 1st Illinois Light Artillery—Lieutenant Joseph A. McCarthey

DIVISION	BRIGADE	REGIMENTS AND OTHERS
6th Division Brigadier General Richard W. Johnson	1st Brigade Colonel Thomas J. Harrison	16th Illinois—Major Charles H. Beeres 5th Iowa—Lieutenant Colonel Harlon Baird 7th Ohio—Colonel Israel Garrard
	2nd Brigade Colonel James Biddle	14th Illinois—Major Haviland Tompkins 6th Indiana—Major Jacob S. Stephens 8th Michigan—Colonel Elisha Mix 3rd Tennessee—Major Benjamin Cunningham
	Artillery	Battery I, 4th United States—Lieutenant Frank G. Smith
7th Division Brigadier General Joseph F. Knipe	1st Brigade Brigadier General John H. Hammond	9th Indiana—Colonel George W. Jackson 10th Indiana—Lieutenant Colonel Benjamin Q.A. Gresham 19th Pennsylvania—Lieutenant Colonel Joseph C. Hess 2nd Tennessee—Lieutenant Colonel William R. Cook 4th Tennessee—Lieutenant Colonel Jacob M. Thornburgh
	2nd Brigade Colonel Gilbert M. L. Johnson	12th Indiana—Colonel Edward Anderson 13th Indiana—Lieutenant Colonel William T. Pepper 6th Tennessee—Colonel Fielding Hurst
	Artillery	14th Battery, Ohio Light—Lieutenant William C. Myers

ARMY OF TENNESSEE
General John B. Hood, Commanding

LEE'S CORPS
Lieutenant General Stephen D. Lee

DIVISION	BRIGADE	REGIMENTS AND OTHERS
Johnson's Division Major General Edward Johnson (c)	Deas's Brigade Brigadier General Zachariah C. Deas	19th Alabama—Lieutenant Colonel Geo. R. Kimbrough 22nd Alabama—Captain H. W. Henry 25th Alabama—Captain Napoleon B. Rouse 39th Alabama—Lieutenant Colonel William C. Clifton 50th Alabama—Colonel John G. Coltart
	Sharp's Brigade Brigadier General Jacob H. Sharp	7th and 9th Mississippi—Major Henry Pope 10th and 44th Mississippi, 9th Sharpshooters Battalion—Captain Robert A. Bell 41st Mississippi—Captain James M. Hicks
	Manigault's Brigade Lieutenant Colonel William L. Butler	24th Alabama—Captain Thomas J. Kimbell 28th Alabama—Captain William M. Nabors 34th Alabama—Lieutenant Colonel John C. Carter 10th South Carolina—Lieutenant Colonel C. Irvine Walker 19th South Carolina—Captain Thomas W. Getzen
	Brantley's Brigade Brigadier General William F. Brantley	24th and 34th Mississippi—Captain Clifton Dancy 27th Mississippi—Captain Samuel M. Pegg 29th and 30th Mississippi—Captain R.W. Williamson Dismounted Cavalry—Captain D.W. Alexander
	Courtney's Artillery Battalion Captain James P. Douglas	Dent's (Alabama) Battery—Captain Staunton H. Dent Douglas's (Texas) Battery—Lieutenant Ben. Hardin Garrity's (Alabama) Battery—Lieutenant Henry F. Carrell

DIVISION	BRIGADE	REGIMENTS AND OTHERS
Stevenson's Division Major General Carter L. Stevenson	Cumming's Brigade Colonel Elihu P. Watkins	34th Georgia—Captain Russell A. Jones 36th Georgia—Colonel Charles E. Broyles 39th Georgia—Captain William P. Milton 56th Georgia—Captain Benjamin T. Spearman
	Pettus's Brigade Brigadier General Edmund W. Pettus	20th Alabama—Colonel James M. Dedman 23rd Alabama—Lieutenant Colonel Joseph B. Bibb 30th Alabama—Lieutenant Colonel James K. Elliott 31st Alabama—Lieutenant Colonel Thomas M. Arrington 46th Alabama—Captain George E. Brewer
	Brown's and Reynolds's Brigade Colonel Joseph B. Palmer (on detached service at Murfreesboro)	60th North Carolina—Major James T. Huff 3rd and 18th Tennessee—Lieutenant Colonel William R. Butler 23rd, 26th and 45th Tennessee—Colonel Anderson Searcy 32nd Tennessee—Colonel John P. McGuire 54th Virginia Infantry—Captain William G. Anderson 63rd Virginia Infantry—Lieutenant Colonel Connally H. Lynch

DIVISION	BRIGADE	REGIMENTS AND OTHERS
Clayton's Division Major General Henry D. Clayton	Stovall's Brigade Brigadier General Marcellus A. Stovall	40th Georgia—Colonel Abda Johnson 41st Georgia—Captain Jared E. Stallings 42nd Georgia—Colonel Robert J. Henderson 43rd Georgia—Colonel Henry C. Kellogg 52nd Georgia—Captain Rufus R. Asbury
	Holtzclaw's Brigade Brigadier General James T. Holtzclaw	18th Alabama—Lieutenant Colonel Peter F. Hunley 32nd and 58th Alabama—Colonel Bushrod Jones 36th Alabama—Captain Nathan M. Carpenter 38th Alabama—Captain Charles E. Bussey
	Gibson's Brigade Brigadier General Randall L. Gibson	1st Louisiana—Captain J. C. Stafford 4th Louisiana—Colonel Samuel E. Hunter 13th Louisiana—Lieutenant Colonel Francis L. Campbell 16th Louisiana—Lieutenant Colonel Robert H. Lindsey 19th Louisiana—Major Camp Flournoy 20th Louisiana—Captain Alexander Dresel 25th Louisiana—Colonel Francis C. Zacharie 30th Louisiana—Major Arthur Picolet 4th Louisiana Battalion—Captain T.A. Bisland 14th Louisiana Battalion Sharpshooters— Lieutenant A.T. Martin
	Eldridge's Artillery Battalion Captain Charles E. Fenner	Eufaula (Alabama) Battery—Captain William J. McKenzie Fenner's (Louisiana) Battery—Lieutenant W.T. Cluverius Stanford's (Mississippi) Battery—Lieutenant James S. McCall
Corps Artillery Major John W. Johnston	Johnston's Battalion Captain John B. Rowan	Corput's (Georgia) Battery—Lieutenant William S. Hoge Marshall's (Tennessee) Battery—Captain Lucius G. Marshall Stephens (Georgia) Light Artillery— Lieutenant William L. Ritter

STEWART'S CORPS
Lieutenant General Alexander P. Stewart

DIVISION	BRIGADE	REGIMENTS AND OTHERS
Loring's Division Major General William W. Loring	Featherston's Brigade Brigadier General Winfield S. Featherston	1st Mississippi—Captain Owen D. Hughes 3rd Mississippi—Captain O.H. Johnston 22nd Mississippi—Major Martin A. Oatis 31st Mississippi—Captain Robert A. Collins 33rd Mississippi—Captain T.L. Cooper 40th Mississippi—Colonel Wallace B. Colbert 1st Mississippi Battalion—Major James M. Stigler
	Adams's Brigade Colonel Robert Lowry	6th Mississippi—Lieutenant Colonel Thomas J. Borden 14th Mississippi—Colonel Washington L. Doss 15th Mississippi—Lieutenant Colonel James R. Binford 20th Mississippi—Major Thomas B. Graham 23rd Mississippi—Major George W. B. Garrett 43rd Mississippi—Colonel Richard Harrison
	Scott's Brigade Colonel John Snodgrass	55th Alabama—Major James B. Dickey 57th Alabama—Major J. Horatio Wiley 27th, 35th and 49th Alabama—Lieutenant Colonel John D. Weeden 12th Louisiana—Captain James T. Davi
	Myrick's Artillery Battalion Lieutenant Colonel S.C. Williams	Bouanchaud's (Louisiana) Battery Cowan's (Mississippi) Battery Darden's (Mississippi) Battery

Division	Brigade	Regiments and Others
French's Division Major Samuel G. French was not present during the battle due to a severe eye infection, and the division was temporarily attached to Walthall's Division	Sears's Brigade Brigadier General Claudius W. Sears (w)	4th Mississippi 35th Mississippi 36th Mississippi 39th Mississippi 46th Mississippi 7th Mississippi Battalion
	Ector's Brigade Colonel David Coleman	29th North Carolina—Major Ezekiel H. Hampton 39th North Carolina—Captain James G. Crawford 9th Texas—Major James H. McReynolds 10th Texas Cavalry (dismounted)—Colonel C.R. Earp 14th Texas Cavalry (dismounted)—Captain Robert H. Harkey 32nd Texas Cavalry (dismounted)—Major William E. Estes
	Cockrell's Brigade (on detached duty on the Duck River) Colonel Peter C. Flournoy	1st and 4th Missouri—Captain James H. Wickersham 2nd and 6th Missouri—Lieutenant Colonel Stephen Cooper 3rd and 5th Missouri—Captain Benjamin E. Guthrie 1st Regiment, 3rd Battalion Missouri Cavalry (dismounted)—Lieutenant C.B. Cleveland
Storrs's Artillery Battalion	Guibor's (Missouri) Battery Hoskins's (Mississippi) Battery Kolb's (Alabama) Battery	

Division	Brigade	Regiments and Others
Walthall's Division Major General Edward C. Walthall	Quarles's Brigade Brigadier General George D. Johnston	1st Alabama—Lieutenant Charles M. McRae 42nd, 46th, 49th, 53rd and 55th Tennessee—Captain Austin M. Duncan 48th Tennessee—Colonel William M. Voorhies
	Cantey's Brigade Brigadier General Charles M. Shelley	17th Alabama—Captain John Bolling Jr. 26th Alabama—Captain D.M. Gideon 29th Alabama—Captain Samuel Abernethy 37th Mississippi—Major Samuel H. Terral
	Reynolds's Brigade Brigadier General Daniel H. Reynolds	1st Arkansas Mounted Rifles (dismounted)—Captain R.P. Parks 2nd Arkansas Mounted Rifles (dismounted)—Major James P. Eagle 4th Arkansas—Major Jesse A. Ross 9th Arkansas—Captain W. L. Phifer 25th Arkansas—Lieutenant T.J. Edwards
	Trueheart's Artillery Battalion Captain James H. Yates	Lumsden's (Alabama) battery Selden's (Alabama) battery Tarrant's (Alabama) battery

Cheatham's Corps
Major General Benjamin F. Cheatham

Chief of Artillery
Colonel Melancthon Smith

Division	Brigade	Regiments and Others
Brown's Division Brigadier General Mark P. Lowrey	Gist's Brigade Lieutenant Colonel Zachariah L. Watters	46th Georgia—Captain Malcolm Gillis 65th Georgia, 8th Georgia Battalion—Captain William W. Grant 2nd Georgia Sharpshooters Battalion—Captain William H. Brown 16th South Carolina—Captain John W. Boling 24th South Carolina—Captain W. C. Griffith
	Strahl's Brigade Colonel Andrew J. Kellar	4th, 5th, 31st, 33rd and 38th Tennessee—Lieutenant Colonel Luke W. Finlay 19th, 24th and 41st Tennessee—Captain Daniel A. Kennedy
	Maney's Brigade Colonel Hume R. Field	4th (P.A.), 6th, 9th and 50th Tennessee—Lieutenant Colonel George W. Pease 1st and 27th Tennessee—Lieutenant Colonel John L. House 8th, 16th and 28th Tennessee—Colonel John H. Anderson
	Vaughan's Brigade Colonel William M. Watkins	11th and 29th Tennessee—Major John E. Binns 12th and 47th Tennessee—Captain C.N. Wade 13th, 51st, 52nd and 154th Tennessee—Major John T. Williamson
	Artillery Battalion	Perry's (Florida) Battery Phelan's (Alabama) Battery Turner's (Mississippi) Battery

DIVISION	BRIGADE	REGIMENTS AND OTHERS
Cleburne's Division Brigadier General James A. Smith	Smith's Brigade Colonel Charles H. Olmstead (attached to Forrest's command at Murfreesboro)	1st Georgia Volunteers—Major Martin J. Ford 54th Georgia—Captain George W. Moody 57th Georgia—Captain Lucius C. Bryan 63rd Georgia—Captain Elijah J. Craven
	Govan's Brigade Brigadier General Daniel C. Govan	1st, 2nd, 5th, 13th, 15th and 24th Arkansas—Colonel Peter V. Green 6th and 7th Arkansas—Lieutenant Colonel Peter Snyder 8th and 19th Arkansas—Major David H. Hamiter
	Lowrey's Brigade Lieutenant Colonel Robert H. Abercrombie	16th, 33rd and 45th Alabama—Lieutenant Colonel Robert H. Abercrombie 5th Mississippi, 3rd Mississippi Battalion—Captain F.M. Woodward 8th and 32nd Mississippi—Major Andrew E. Moody
	Granbury's Brigade Captain E.T. Broughton	5th Confederate—Lieutenant William E. Smith 35th Tennessee—Colonel Benjamin J. Hill 6th and 15th Texas—Captain Benjamin R. Tyus 7th Texas—Captain O.P. Forrest 10th Texas—Captain R. D. Kennedy 17th and 18th Texas Cavalry (dismounted)—Captain F.L. McKnight 24th and 25th Texas Cavalry (dismounted)—Captain John F. Matthews Nutt's (Louisiana) Cavalry Company (dismounted)—Captain L.M. Nutt

DIVISION	BRIGADE	REGIMENTS AND OTHERS
Bate's Division Major General William B. Bate	Tyler's Brigade Brigadier General Thomas B. Smith (captured and then wounded while in custody)	37th Georgia—Captain James A. Sanders 4th Georgia Sharpshooters Battalion—Major Theodore D. Caswell 2nd, 10th, 20th and 37th Tennessee— Lieutenant Colonel William M. Shy
	Finley's Brigade Major Jacob A. Lash	1st and 3rd Florida—Captain Matthew H. Strain 6th Florida—Captain Angus McMillan 7th Florida—Captain Robert B. Smith 1st Florida Cavalry and 4th Florida Infantry— Captain George R. Langford
	Jackson's Brigade Brigadier General Henry R. Jackson (c)	1st Georgia (Confederate) and 66th Georgia— Lieutenant Colonel James C. Gordon 25th Georgia—Captain Joseph E. Fulton 29th and 30th Georgia—Colonel William D. Mitchell 1st Georgia Sharpshooters Battalion— Lieutenant R.C. King
	Artillery Battalion Captain R.T. Beauregard	Slocomb's (Louisiana) Battery Ferguson's (South Carolina) Battery Mebane's (Tennessee) Battery
Corps Artillery	Hotchkiss's Battalion	Bledsoe's (Missouri) Battery Goldthwaite's (Alabama) Battery Key's (Arkansas) Battery
	Cobb's Battalion	Ferguson's (South Carolina) Battery Phillips's [Mebane's] (Tennessee) Battery Slocomb's (Louisiana) Battery

CAVALRY CORPS

Major General Nathan B. Forrest (detached; at Murfreesboro with Jackson's and Buford's Divisions)

DIVISION	BRIGADE	REGIMENTS AND OTHERS
Chalmers's Division Brigadier General James R. Chalmers	Rucker's Brigade Colonel Edmund W. Rucker (w and c) Lieutenant Colonel R.R. White	7th Alabama Cavalry 5th Mississippi Cavalry 3rd Tennessee Cavalry (Forrest's Old Regiment) 7th Tennessee Cavalry 12th Tennessee Cavalry 14th Tennessee Cavalry 15th Tennessee Cavalry
	Biffle's Brigade Colonel Jacob B. Biffle	4th Tennessee Cavalry 9th Tennessee Cavalry 10th Tennessee Cavalry
Buford's Division (detached; at Murfreesboro) Brigadier General Abraham Buford	Bell's Brigade Colonel Tyree H. Bell	2nd/22nd Tennessee Cavalry (Barteau's) 19th Tennessee Cavalry 20th Tennessee Cavalry 21st Tennessee Cavalry Nixon's Tennessee Cavalry Regiment
	Crossland's Brigade Colonel Edward Crossland	3rd Kentucky Mounted Infantry 7th Kentucky Mounted Infantry 8th Kentucky Mounted Infantry 12th Kentucky Cavalry Huey's Kentucky Battalion
Jackson's Division (detached; at Murfreesboro) Brigadier General William H. Jackson	Armstrong's Brigade Brigadier General Frank C. Armstrong	1st Mississippi Cavalry 2nd Mississippi Cavalry 28th Mississippi Cavalry Ballentine's Mississippi Regiment
	Ross's Brigade Brigadier General Lawrence S. Ross	3rd Texas Cavalry 6th Texas Cavalry 9th Texas Cavalry 27th Texas Cavalry 1st Texas Legion
	Artillery	Morton's Tennessee Battery

Notes

Prologue

1. Smith, *In the Lion's Mouth*, 226.
2. Hood, *John Bell Hood*, 75.
3. Wellington's actual quote was: "It has been…the nearest run thing you ever saw."

Chapter 1

4. Davis's first wife, Sarah Knox Taylor, died of malaria three months after they were married in 1835.
5. For more details of the events surrounding the selection of John Bell Hood to replace Joseph E. Johnson as commander of the Army of Tennessee, see Connelly, *Autumn of Glory*, 391–426.
6. This incident was graphically depicted in the 1939 movie *Gone with the Wind*.
7. Some have argued that the Army of Tennessee would have fared better during its Tennessee Campaign if Hardee's old corps had been given to Major General Patrick Cleburne instead of Frank Cheatham. Cleburne was known as perhaps the best division commander in the Western Theater, but he had little experience in command at corps level. Cleburne, an Irishman, had also voiced some very unpopular opinions about offering freedom to slaves in return for military service. Finally,

Cleburne was six months junior to Cheatham as a major general. By choosing Cheatham, President Davis avoided another seniority issue like the one between Hood and Hardee and still got a solid soldier who had already commanded the corps temporarily on several occasions and was, by all rights, next in line for the job. Whether Cleburne would have done a better job in the campaign is impossible to know.

8. While presumably submitting this new plan for Beauregard's approval, Hood had already notified both Richmond and General Richard Taylor, the commander of the department he was about to enter, that he was on the way.

9. Elliott, *Soldier of Tennessee*, 223.

Chapter 2

10. Jacobson and Rupp, *For Cause and for Country*, 58–59.

11. Knight, *Battle of Franklin*, 29.

12. Beauregard hoped to have Hood on the way by November 9. Jacobson and Rupp, *For Cause and for Country*, 58.

13. This was Brigadier General Abraham Buford's division. Jordan and Pryor, *Campaigns of General Nathan Bedford Forrest*, 608.

14. Obtaining accurate numbers for Civil War armies has always been a problem. Jacobson and Rupp, in *For Cause and for Country* (page 529), the latest and, in my opinion, best study of the first part of the campaign, gives Hood's total effective strength at the beginning of the campaign as thirty-three thousand. There were, of course, other support and logistic troops that took part in the campaign, but the fighting men probably numbered about thirty-three thousand.

15. Croxton and his brigade were patrolling the north side of the Tennessee River when Hood arrived. Within a week or so, they were joined by Hatch and Capron, with Hatch in overall command.

16. Over the next two weeks, additional infantry and cavalry units would arrive, bringing the Federal strength at Spring Hill and Franklin up to almost thirty-one thousand.

Chapter 3

17. *The War of the Rebellion: A Compilation of the Official Records of the Union and Confederate Armies* (hereafter noted as *OR*) 45: 340, 378 and 670. (All *OR* references are from Volume 45, Series 1, Part I, unless otherwise stated). Colonel Silas Strickland had been in Columbia with two Federal regiments since November 13. On the twenty-third, another regiment arrived, and a few hours before dawn on the twenty-fourth, Colonel Orlando Moore's brigade began unloading from rail cars, having come from Johnsonville. All told, they would have probably numbered twice Chalmers's force. S.D. Lee's corps, the lead Confederate infantry troops, did not arrive at Columbia until the twenty-sixth.

18. *OR* 45: 557. Wilson's own estimate of the strength of Schofield's cavalry when he took command on November 23 was 4,300 men. During the next week, additional regiments would arrive that would add at least 1,000 more men, bringing the Federal cavalry strength at Franklin to over 5,000. During the same time, Wilson estimated that Forrest had at least 10,000 men—about twice his actual strength. In fact, from Columbia on, the Confederate and Federal cavalry numbers were about evenly matched—give or take a few hundred. The Confederates had the edge in experience and leadership, but the Federals had the edge in equipment, with many units armed with seven-shot Spencer carbines.

19. Jordan and Pryor, *Campaigns of General Nathan Bedford Forrest*, 53–54.

20. The commander in question was Braxton Bragg in the fall of 1863, and the junior officer was Lieutenant A.W. Gould, one of Forrest's artillery officers. Gould took exception to being transferred, and on June 14, 1863, he walked into Forrest's headquarters in Columbia, Tennessee, and shot his commander in the hip. Forrest then stabbed Gould with his penknife. Forrest recovered, but Lieutenant Gould bled to death.

21. For Major Young's account and accompanying map, see *OR* 45: 604.

22. For Wilson's communication with Schofield on the twenty-eighth, see *OR* 45: 1,109–13. For Wilson's advice to fall back on Spring Hill, see *OR* 45: 1,143.

23. *OR* 45: 1,113–44.

24. This information came from Colonel Sidney Post, who had been sent with his brigade to check out reports of Confederate troop movements. See Jacobson and Rupp, *For Cause and for Country*, 108–09.

Chapter 4

25. The Martin Cheairs home is now called Ferguson Hall and is owned by the Tennessee Children's Home. It can be seen by appointment.
26. Jacobson and Rupp, *For Cause and for Country*, 119–20. The troops that came in from the west were the Third Illinois and a few companies of the Eleventh Indiana.
27. Ibid., 121. Although outnumbered, most of the Federal troops were significantly better armed with Colt revolving rifles and Maynard breechloaders. The Second Michigan had seven-shot Spencer carbines.
28. For Ross's account of this action, see *OR* 45: 760–70.
29. Jacobson and Rupp, *For Cause and for Country*, 129.
30. This was just north of the intersection of present-day Saturn Parkway and Kedron Road.
31. The exact wording of Cleburne's orders is not known. Cleburne was killed about twenty-four hours later and left no record. These, however, were the orders personally given by Hood to Major General William Bate a few minutes later. They are likely the same thing that Cleburne was told. See Bate's report in *OR* 45: 742.
32. *OR* 45: 267–69. Report of Brigadier General Luther P. Bradley, who was wounded during the engagement.
33. Ibid., 113, 267–69, 275. After Luther Bradley was wounded, command of his brigade passed to Colonel Joseph Conrad of the Fifteenth Missouri. The brigade, under Conrad, would play a key role the next day at Franklin.
34. Some members of Granbury's brigade were within two hundred yard of the pike.
35. See note 29.
36. Jacobson and Rupp, *For Cause and for Country*, 160. What Brown didn't know was that this was a small part of John Q. Lane's Federal line and no real threat to Brown's attack. See also Brown's statement in 1881 in *Southern Historical Society Papers* 9, 538.
37. Jacobson and Rupp, *For Cause and for Country*, 157.
38. *Southern Historical Society Papers* 9, 526, 530. Cheatham claims that, at this meeting, Hood decided to postpone the attack on the town until the morning. Hood denies this.
39. Ibid., 541. Statement of Major General William B. Bate in 1881.

Chapter 5

40. Major General Thomas Ruger's division was seriously understrength, having only two brigades. His first brigade under Brigadier General J.A. Cooper was on detached duty near Centerville.

41. *OR* 45: 1,138. In later years, John Schofield would downplay the seriousness of his army's position at Spring Hill that night, claiming that he had the situation well in hand. When David Stanley read Schofield's version of Spring Hill over thirty years later, he pronounced it "the merest bosh!" Schofield's dispatch that Captain William J. Twining sent to headquarters from Franklin at 10:00 p.m., having ridden from Thompson Station on Schofield's orders, doesn't sound very confident. One line from Twining's message to George Thomas reads, "He [Schofield] regards his situation as extremely perilous and fears that he will be forced into a general battle tomorrow or lose his wagon train."

42. A.P. Stewart's report, *OR* 45: 713.

43. Ross's report, *OR* 45, 770.

44. Captain W.O. Dodd as quoted in *Southern Historical Society Papers* 9, 522. The truth about the events of the afternoon and evening of November 29, 1864, is much more elusive, complicated and disputed than this brief account can possibly cover. In my opinion, the two best and most current accounts and analysis of Spring Hill are found in Jacobson and Rupp, *For Cause and for Country* (pages 141–212) and Gillum, *Twenty-Five Hours to Tragedy*.

45. Gillum, *Twenty-Five Hours to Tragedy*, 416.

Chapter 6

46. Cox, *Battle of Franklin*, 38–39. Cox and his men had been on duty, guarding the Duck River at Columbia, during the previous day and had then marched twenty-two miles in the last twelve hours. A short rest was certainly in order.

47. Schofield had used pontoons to cross the Duck River at Columbia but did not have the wagons available to haul them with him during his retreat to Franklin, hence the request to Nashville for more pontoons to use at Franklin. George Thomas, in Nashville, might not have understood that Schofield had been unable to bring his pontoons from Columbia and therefore needed replacements at Franklin as soon as possible.

48. Cox, *Battle of Franklin*, 39.

49. BOFT (Battle of Franklin Trust) archives, Carter House collection.

50. *OR* 45: 431–32. Giles J. Cockerill, the chief of the XXIII Corps artillery (also commanded Battery D of the First Ohio Volunteer Light Artillery).
51. Ibid., 1,169.
52. Ibid., 1,170. Schofield to Thomas.
53. Ibid., 352. Cox says that he received this order at about 2:00 p.m.
54. Ibid., 115.
55. For details of the Federal position at Franklin, see Cox, *Battle of Franklin*, 37–63.
56. *OR* 45: 736. Report of Colonel Ellison Capers.
57. BOFT, Carnton collection. A McGavock family story says that Forrest entered the house and viewed the Federal lines from a second-floor landing over the back porch. The cover of this book depicts Forrest and a staff officer riding away from Carnton, as painted by artist John Paul Strain.
58. Hurst, *Nathan Bedford Forrest*, 233.
59. For a more detailed discussion of Hood's meeting, see Jacobson and Rupp, *For Cause and for Country*, 289–96.
60. Because he remained at Columbia to try to hold the bulk of Schofield's army at the Duck River while Hood cut them off at Spring Hill on the twenty-ninth, S.D. Lee's three divisions brought up the rear of the Confederate column on the march from Spring Hill to Franklin on the thirtieth. Most of Hood's artillery had remained at Columbia with Lee and was still with him at the rear of the column. The first of Lee's divisions (Ed Johnson) did not arrive on the field at Franklin until 5:00 p.m. and was the only one of Lee's units engaged, going in at about 7:00 p.m., two hours after dark.
61. For a complete discussion of the question of Hood and liquor or drugs, see Hood, *John Bell Hood*, 267–80.
62. *OR* 45: 742–43. Bate reported that he received his orders at about 3:00 p.m.
63. Schofield, *Forty-Six Years in the Army*, 184.
64. Conrad and Lane's brigades together numbered almost three thousand men. Like the skirmishers from the other regiments, they expected to be ordered to fall back in the face of a general assault, as their position that far in front of the main works would be completely unsupported.

Chapter 7

65. Report of Major General E.C. Walthall, *OR* 45: 720.

66. There are several different versions of Brigadier General Adams's charge and subsequent death. For a more detailed discussion of this incident, see Jacobson and Rupp, *For Cause and for Country*, 421–31.

67. Scofield, *Retreat from Pulaski to Nashville*, 41; Jacobson and Rupp, *For Cause and for Country*, 351.

68. Jacobson and Rupp, *For Cause and for Country*, 294–96, 300.

69. *OR* 45: 270 (Conrad report). Joseph Conrad reported that orders to retire to the main line did come a little later, when Wagner finally realized what was happening, but that the enemy was so close by that time that he feared his men would panic during the withdrawal.

70. *OR* 45: 256, 271. Both Conrad and Lane insist that it was the other brigade that broke first.

71. Knight, *Battle of Franklin*, 78.

72. George W. Gordon as quoted in *Confederate Veteran* (January 1900), 7.

73. James Barr, Company E, Sixty-fifth Illinois. BOFT, Carter House collection.

74. As an example of how intense the fight was along the line of the 104th Ohio in front of the cotton gin, six of the eleven Medals of Honor awarded for valor at Franklin went to members of the 104th.

75. Major General Cleburne was the highest-ranking officer killed during the campaign.

76. For a detailed discussion of casualties at Franklin, see Jacobson and Rupp, *For Cause and for Country*, 516–22.

77. The home of Albert and Margaretha Lotz still stands on Columbia Avenue in Franklin and is a Civil War museum. See http://lotzhouse.com.

78. BOFT, Carter House collection.

79. Ibid. Captain Theodrick "Tod" Carter, son of Fountain Branch Carter, who owned the Carter House, is sometimes confused with Brigadier General John C. Carter, one of John C. Brown's brigade commanders, who was also mortally wounded during the battle. Brigadier General Carter is not related to the family who owned the Carter House.

80. *OR* 45: 761.

81. Ibid., 691.

82. D.H. Patterson, First Alabama, as quoted in *Confederate Veteran* (March, 1901), 117.

83. Adam J. Weaver, 104th Ohio, BOFT, Carter House collection.

Chapter 8

84. *OR* 45, Part II: 628 (Hood's Field Order #38, congratulating his troops on their "victory" at Franklin); *OR* 45: 654. In this report, written two and a half months after the battle, Hood gives his losses at Franklin as 4,500, which probably understates his actual losses by about 35 percent.

85. James S. Pressnall, from an undated memoir courtesy of Kathryn Crawford, Pressnall's great-great-granddaughter.

86. Lieutenant Thomas C. Thoburn, Fiftieth Ohio, as quoted in Logsdon, *Eyewitnesses at the Battle of Franklin*, 63.

87. *OR* 45: 969.

88. Losson, *Tennessee's Forgotten Warriors*, 227.

89. Jacobson and Rupp, *For Cause and for Country*, 508.

90. For a detailed discussion of the Federal and Confederate casualties at Franklin, see Jacobson and Rupp, *For Cause and for Country,* 516–24.

91. Knight, *Battle of Franklin*, 97.

92. Hood, *Advance and Retreat*, 299–300.

93. For a criticism of Hood's decision, see Sword, *The Confederacy's Last Hurrah*, 279–80. For a defense of Hood's decision, see Hood, *John Bell Hood*, 176–84.

94. Owens' Crossroads is not mentioned in Hammond's official report, but the regimental histories of four of his five regiments claim they were there.

95. *OR* 45: 744 (Bate's report). Murfreesboro was, in fact, held by almost eight thousand men under the command of Major General Lovell H. Rousseau.

96. In addition to Schofield's troops and A.J. Smith's XVI Corps, about five thousand more men had arrived on the evening of the first from Chattanooga.

97. *OR* 45: 615–16 (Milroy's report) and 755 (Forrest's report).

98. Ibid., 764 (Chalmers's report).

99. Logsdon, *Eyewitnesses at the Battle of Nashville*, 30–31.

100. Ibid., 33.

101. *OR* 45, Part II, 15–18.

102. Ibid., 17–18, 70 (Thomas to Grant, evening of December 2 and December 6).

103. Ibid., 70.

104. Logsdon, *Eyewitnesses at the Battle of Nashville,* 24 (Corporal Edgar Jones, Eighteenth Alabama).

105. Ibid., 26 (William Worsham, Nineteenth Tenneesee).
106. Watkins, *Co. Aytch*, 265. "Cheatham's division," which Watkins refers to, was Frank Cheatham's old division, which, at Franklin, was commanded by John C. Brown and had, indeed, lost all its general officers. At Nashville, it was commanded by Brigadier General Mark P. Lowrey, who had come over from Cleburne's division.
107. *OR* 45, Part II: 114–16 (text of order relieving Thomas and communication between Grant and Halleck).
108. Ibid., 230 (Logan to Grant).
109. Logsdon, *Eyewitnesses at the Battle of Nashville*, 40.
110. *OR* 45, Part II: 180, 183–84 (Thomas to Henry Halleck and Special Field Order #342).

Chapter 9

111. William Stahl, Forty-ninth Ohio, as quoted in Logsdon, *Eyewitnesses at the Battle of Nashville*, 44.
112. McDonough, *Nashville*, 166.
113. *OR* 45: 765–66.
114. What Coleman probably saw was Brigadier General John McArthur's division of infantry on their way to their attack positions and Datus Coon's brigade of cavalry.
115. *OR* 45: 765 (Chalmers's report).
116. At this point, A.P. Stewart's corps had only two divisions. Major General Samuel G. French was on sick leave, so his three small brigades were reassigned. Cockrell's Missouri brigade, almost destroyed at Franklin, was on detached duty while Ector's and Sears's brigades had been attached to Walthall.
117. *OR* 45: 128–29 (Wood's report).
118. McDonough, *Nashville*, 190.
119. Logsdon, *Eyewitnesses at the Battle of Nashville*, 56.
120. *OR* 45: 446 (Hubbard's report).
121. McDonough, *Nashville*, 203. Colonel Sylvester G. Hill, Thirty-fifth Iowa, was the highest-ranking Federal officer killed at Nashville.
122. Ibid., 207.
123. *OR* 45, Part II: 115.

Chapter 10

124. *OR* 45: 705 (Brigadier General James T. Holtzclaw, CSA, on his brigade's defense of Peach Orchard Hill).
125. See www.bonps.org/shys-hill.
126. *OR* 45: 744. Two weeks earlier, as he moved to Murfreesboro, Bate listed his strength at 1,600 men.
127. I would like to thank Brian Allison, former historian at Traveler's Rest Historic Site in Nashville, for the strength numbers used for the forces at Nashville.
128. Logsdon, *Eyewitnesses at the Battle of Nashville*, 70.
129. *OR* 45: 701 (Stovall's report).
130. McDonough, *Nashville*, 222.
131. Ibid., 226.
132. *OR* 45: 705 (Holtzclaw's report).
133. Article by Ambrose Bierce in the June 5, 1898 *San Francisco Examiner*.
134. *OR* 45, Part II: 215 (Schofield to Thomas).
135. See www.civilwarinteractive.com/Biographies/BiosThomasBentonSmith.htm.
136. *OR* 45: 689 (S.D. Lee's report).
137. Ibid., 765–66 (Chalmers's report).
138. Ibid., 552 (Wilson's report).
139. McDonough, *Nashville*, 262–63.
140. *OR* 45: 756 (Forrest's report).

Chapter 11

141. W.O. Dodd, *Southern Historical Society Papers* 9 (1881), 523.
142. Logsdon, *Eyewitnesses at the Battle of Nashville*, 108–09.
143. Watkins, *Co. Aytch*, 269.
144. *OR* 45, Part II: 210.
145. Ibid., 222 (Wilson to R.W. Johnson).
146. Smith, *In the Lion's Mouth*, 107.
147. Captain George E. Brewer, Forty-sixth Alabama, *Confederate Veteran* 18, no. 7 (July 1910), 327. Captain Brewer also states that many of their own (Confederate) cavalry were wearing captured blue Federal overcoats so that it was difficult to tell them from the real Federal cavalry.

148. *OR* 45: 699 (Clayton report). With the exception of one unit, Clayton has nothing good to say about the performance of Chalmers's cavalry on December 17.
149. *OR* 45, Part II: 237.
150. *OR* 45: 690 (S.D. Lee's report).
151 For a more detailed account of the fight at Little Harpeth, see Smith, *In the Lion's Mouth*, 121–27. See also *OR* 45: 696 (Stevenson's report).
152. Smith, *In the Lion's Mouth*, 136.

Chapter 12

153. Ibid., 154.
154. *OR* 45: 161 (journal of the IV corps).
155. Ibid., 160 (journal of the IV corps); Jordan and Pryor, *Campaigns of General Nathan Bedford Forrest*, 646. The night of December 19–20 was said to have been cold "beyond the experience of anyone with Hood's army."
156. Jordan and Pryor, *Campaigns of General Nathan Bedford Forrest*, 646.
157. *OR* 45: 162 (journal of the IV Corps).
158. Ibid., 673 (journal of the Army of Tennessee).
159. This position is located in a small pass through some hills about six miles south of the Duck River on today's U.S. 31.
160. Smith, *In the Lion's Mouth*, 178.
161. *OR* 45: 673 (journal of the Army of Tennessee).
162. *OR* 45, Part II: 334 (Wilson to Thomas's headquarters).
163. *Confederate Veteran* 2, no. 2 (February 1894) 46–47.
164. *OR* 45, Part II: 342 (Wilson to Thomas).
165. *OR* 45: 772.
166. *OR* 45, Part II: 371.
167. Jordan and Pryor, *Campaigns of General Nathan Bedford Forrest*, 651.
168. Ibid., 653.
169. Smith, *In the Lion's Mouth*, 227 (Colonel W.D. Gale, Stewart's staff).

Epilogue

170. Jacobson and Rupp, *For Cause and for Country*, 530–31.
171. *OR* 45: 170.
172. McDonough, *Nashville*, 264.

Sources and Recommended Reading

Bobrick, Benson. *Master of War: The Life of General George H. Thomas*. New York: Simon and Schuster, 2009.

Connelly, Thomas L. *Autumn of Glory: The Army of Tennessee, 1862–1865*. Baton Rouge: Louisiana State University Press, 1971.

Cox, Jacob. *The Battle of Franklin Tennessee, November 30, 1864: A Monograph*. Dayton, OH: Kessinger Publishing, 1983.

Daniel, Larry. *Soldiering in the Army of Tennessee: A Portrait of Life in a Confederate Army*. Chapel Hill: University of North Carolina Press, 1991.

Elliott, Sam Davis. *Soldier of Tennessee: General Alexander P. Stewart and the Civil War in the West*. Baton Rouge: Louisiana State University Press, 1999.

Gillum, Jamie. *Twenty-Five Hours to Tragedy*. Spring Hill, TN: CreateSpace, 2014.

Hood, John Bell. *Advance and Retreat: Personal Experiences in the United States and Confederate States Armies*. Cambridge, MA: Da Capo Press, 1993.

Hood, Stephen M. *John Bell Hood: The Rise, Fall and Resurrection of a Confederate General*. El Dorado Hills, CA: Savas Beatie, 2013.

Hurst, Jack. *Nathan Bedford Forrest: A Biography*. New York: Random House, 1993.

Jacobson, Eric A., and Richard A. Rupp. *Baptism of Fire: The 44th Missouri, 175th Ohio, and 183rd Ohio at the Battle of Franklin*. Franklin, TN: O'More Publishing, 2011.

———. *For Cause and for Country*. Franklin, TN: O'More Publishing, 2007.

Jordan, Thomas, and J.P. Pryor. *The Campaigns of General Nathan Bedford Forrest*. Cambridge, MA: De Capo Press, 1996.

Knight, James R. *The Battle of Franklin: When the Devil Had Full Possession of the Earth*. Charleston, SC: The History Press, 2009.

Logsdon, David, ed. *Eyewitness at the Battle of Franklin*. Nashville TN: Kettle Mills Press, 2000.

Losson, Christopher. *Tennessee's Forgotten Warriors: Frank Cheatham and His Confederate Division*. Knoxville: University of Tennessee Press, 1989.

McDonough, James Lee. *Nashville: The Western Confederacy's Final Gamble*. Knoxville: University of Tennessee Press, 2004.

McDonough, James Lee, and Thomas L. Connelly. *Five Tragic Hours: The Battle of Franklin*. Knoxville: University of Tennessee Press, 1983.

Schofield, John M. *Forty-Six Years in the Army*. New York: Century Co., 1897.

Scofield, Levi T. *The Retreat from Pulaski to Nashville Tennessee*. Reprint. Franklin, TN: Mint Julep Printing Co., 1996.

Smith, Derek. *In the Lion's Mouth: Hoods Tragic Retreat from Nashville, 1864*. Mechanicsburg, PA: Stackpole Books, 2011.

Southern Historical Society Papers.

Stanley, David Sloan. *An American General*. Santa Barbara, CA: Narrative Press, 2003.

Stockdale, Paul H. *The Death of an Army: The Battle of Nashville and Hood's Retreat*. Murfreesboro, TN: Southern Heritage Press, 1992.

Sword, Wiley. *The Confederacy's Last Hurrah: Spring Hill, Franklin and Nashville*. Lawrence: University Press of Kansas, 1993.

U.S. War Department. *The War of the Rebellion: A Compilation of the Official Records of the Union and Confederate Armies*. 128 vols. Washington, D.C.: Government Printing Office, 1900.

Watkins, Sam R. *Co. Aytch*. Edited by Ruth Hill Fulton McAllister. Franklin, TN: Providence House Publishers, 2007.

Zimmerman, Mark. *Guide to Civil War Nashville*. Nashville, TN: Battle of Nashville Preservation Society, 2004.

Index

About the Author

James R. Knight is a graduate of Harding University, class of 1967. He spent five years as a pilot in the U.S. Air Force and thirty-one years as a pilot for Federal Express. In the early '90s, Knight began researching a historical incident in his hometown and published his first work, an article in the *Arkansas Historical Quarterly*, in 1998. In 2003, Eakin Press published his biography of Bonnie and Clyde, titled *Bonnie and Clyde: A Twenty-first-Century Update*. *Hood's Tennessee Campaign* will be his fourth book for The History Press Sesquicentennial Series, the others being on the battles at Franklin and Fort Donelson in Tennessee and Pea Ridge in Arkansas.

Mr. Knight retired from Federal Express in 2004 and lives in Franklin, Tennessee, where he works part time as a historical interpreter for the Battle of Franklin Trust, giving tours of the Carter House historical site. Knight, who refers to himself as a "shade tree historian," is also the coauthor, along with mapmaker Hal Jespersen, of the soon-to-be-published *Grant Rising*, a new map study of the early career of Ulysses S. Grant.

He and his wife, Judy, have been married for forty-six years and have three children and six grandchildren.